BRIDGING THE GAP:

ISLAM'S CHALLENGE FOR AMERICA

ASHRAF W. NUBANI

NEW DEGREE PRESS
COPYRIGHT © 2022 ASHRAF W. NUBANI
All rights reserved.

BRIDGING THE GAP:
Islam's Challenge for America

ISBN	978-1-63730-658-1	Paperback
	978-1-63730-741-0	Kindle Ebook
	978-1-63730-932-2	Ebook

"... Indeed, my prayers, my rites of sacrifice, my living and my dying are for God, Lord of the Worlds."

—QUR'AN 6:162

Contents

INTRODUCTION	11
HOW TO READ THIS BOOK	23
CHAPTER 1. IT DOES ME NO INJURY	33
CHAPTER 2. LET THEM MARRY	53
CHAPTER 3. ZAYD	69
CHAPTER 4. JUSTICE IS NOT RELATIVE	91
CHAPTER 5. FASTING	107
CHAPTER 6. A PALESTINE WE CAN ALL APPLAUD	117
CHAPTER 7. ISLAM AND CHRISTIANITY	141
CHAPTER 8. TERROR REHAB	159
CHAPTER 9. TEAM MEN AND WOMEN	177
CHAPTER 10. ORGANIZED VIOLENCE	193
CHAPTER 11. FOOD IS MEDICINE	205
CHAPTER 12. "YOU SON OF A BLACK SLAVE WOMAN"	217
CONCLUSION	225
ACKNOWLEDGMENTS	233
APPENDIX	235

To the new generation of American youth who have been led to ignore God in the public sphere, who have been unethically represented by our government, who have inherited a nation in unsurmountable debt, but who rise to the challenge by implementing true religion and demonstrate to all that faith can thrive in the free marketplace of ideas, solve our biggest problems, and make the world a better, more just place for all human beings.

Introduction

"Nothing is as powerful as an idea whose time has come..."
—VICTOR HUGO

Reminiscent of the battle scenes of Helms Deep in the *Two Towers* of *The Lord of the Rings* trilogy, documented history in 1187 CE witnessed one of its high points in human events: the liberation of Jerusalem by the Muslim army of Salahuddin. Known in the West as Saladin, he is admired for his generosity, mercy, and chivalry. Like the fictional orcs drooling for "man flesh," the first Christian Crusaders killed, roasted, and ate the flesh of the Muslim inhabitants of Ma'arrat al-Nu'man in modern-day Syria. They did it partly to instill fear and partly out of hunger, as the marauding Crusaders made their way to Jerusalem in 1098 CE (West).

Having satiated their hunger pangs, the purported quest for God and glory led them on to slaughter as many as thirty thousand Muslim and Jewish inhabitants of the city when they took it in 1099 CE (Fordham University). Eighty-eight years later, Salahuddin liberated the city. Retribution, the norm of the day, was expected.

What did he do?

After a negotiated surrender, Salahuddin not only spared the lives of all those in the city, he ransomed those who couldn't afford it with his own wealth (Dajani-Shakeel). He allowed the local Christians to continue to live in the city and worship in peace. His army provided safe passage for those heading to Christian lands. Remarkably, he allowed the exiled Jews to return (Khan).

Reaching further back in history, in the seventh century CE, Islam appeared on the world stage as something strange. Enveloping the two mightiest powers of the time (the Byzantine and the Persian empires), Muslims built some of the largest and most powerful empires known to man. The lasting impact of Islamic civilization on the humanities and sciences, math, inventions, music, and education is undeniable (Sumeyye).

Today, Islam is a challenge for America.

Globally, out of approximately eight billion people on Earth, as many as one-fourth are Muslim. I contend there are two main competitors for the hearts and minds of humanity: the "West" (spearheaded by America) and Islam. America offers the world democracy, individual freedom, and a free market system. Islam offers the best chance for justice in this world with a community of faith—freedom from the confines of a material existence to the expansiveness of an afterlife.

Domestically, Islam had roots in North America before there was an America. Credible, growing evidence shows Muslims discovered the Americas long before Columbus, and Muslims arrived with him to the new world. It is acknowledged that as many as one-sixth of the enslaved population forcibly brought to America was Muslim. Not only is the Muslim presence in America older than the nation itself but Muslim contributions span its entire history. For example, Minnesota Attorney General Keith Ellison, the first Muslim to be elected to Congress, was sworn in on the *Qur'an* owned by Thomas Jefferson.

Arguably, Islam is the fastest growing religion in the US, and it is projected to be the second largest religion after Christianity.

Far from disappearing in the twenty-first century, Islam has reemerged as something strange. Today, it is awkwardly finding its bearings in the face of domestic despotism and Western intervention in Muslim majority countries, and is again making a comeback—politically, socially and economically. The rise of Islam is monitored with trepidation in the West, in particular, by America.

Why?

Islam both presents a challenge for America and challenges America to live up to a universal creed "… that all human beings are created with dignity, that they are endowed by their Creator with certain unalienable Rights, that among these are Life, Liberty and the pursuit of inner peace, contentment and God consciousness."

What is the relationship between America and Islam?

In bombing several Muslim countries, America is in a never-ending "war on terror." The US continues to exploit and siphon natural resources in the Middle East and beyond. We continue to economically and militarily prop-up corrupt authoritarian regimes in the Muslim world at the peril of stoking resentment from the affected populations. Our government continues to defy an international community we engineered (and presumably led) by enabling Israel's seventy-three-year occupation and oppression of the Palestinians.

Ironically, President Trump said of the nation's projected second largest religion: "Islam hates us."

And therein lies the rub.

The US claims to be a role model by virtue of its Western heritage, Christian identity, and American exceptionalism. Yet, innocent Muslims worldwide suffer and are killed because of our policies. I say "our" because if we are a democracy, then "we the people" are ultimately responsible for our nation's actions. By extension, domestically, Muslim Americans are scapegoated for the blowback of our policies.

Objectively, Islam is no more violent than Christianity. The threat of terrorism from Muslims is low (West). Despite these facts, Muslims are discriminated against in the workplace, victimized in hate crimes, singled out at the airports, targeted in FBI-manufactured entrapment cases, and maligned in the media as terrorists. All of these injustices are increasing due to an industry of Islamophobia that preys on ignorance and whips up fear and hatred of Muslims.

For me, growing up as a Muslim immigrant in America meant I was the new kid on the block.

I only experienced obvious Islamophobia for the first time as a law student advocating for prisoners' rights. I was banned from entering a federal prison because the guards decided I resembled one of my clients, who, as destiny would have it, was serving a life sentence for his role in the first World Trade Center bombing. The only "resemblance" was we were both Arab and Muslim.

This experience propelled me on a path of advocacy for civil liberties. This quest for justice and other events in my life—past and present—as a Palestinian, a Muslim, an American, a sermon-giver, an attorney, a son, a husband, a father, and a grandfather obliges me to discharge a sacred trust. I cannot let the animosity of others toward me, Muslims, or the oppressed derail me from acting justly in my beliefs and toward all in society.

Nor can you.

I am compelled to serve as a bridge between Muslims and Americans, Palestinians and Jews, and East and West. The Holy Land, where I come from, is of religious significance to Christians, Muslims, and Jews. Together, we make up over half of the world's population.

In 2015, the Bridge Initiative conducted a comprehensive poll at Georgetown University measuring two decades of American views on Islam and Muslims. The poll concluded "At least one in five Americans has reported unfavorable views of their Muslim compatriots since 2000, and since 1993, the same percentage has reported unfavorable views globally. Today, Americans are as unfamiliar with Islam, as they have been for the past twenty years."

Many Americans hold negative views of Islam as backward and Muslims as violent, but the reality is that we are ignorant about Islam.

As shared human experience intimately knows, and the polls validate, familiarity is one of the greatest antidotes to fear and hatred. Let us come to common terms predicated on honesty, sincerity, and fairness in our dealings with one another. Regardless of one's views on Islam, the fact remains that America owes it to itself to live up to the standards it has set for itself.

Ignorance leaves us dangerously divided. Corruption and greed have created severe economic disparities. We are under the constant threat of one war or another, and the government constantly works to undermine our liberties. Notions of entitlement and racial superiority tear at the fabric of our society.

In addition to fanning the flames of fear and hatred, when former President Trump said "Islam hates us," his administration's policies and the purposefully chosen words implied that Islam can be resisted by force. Islam cannot be defeated on the battlefield. It stands or falls based on its arguments and relevance to people in comparison to other beliefs and ideologies such as those posed by the West, with America at its helm.

What Victor Hugo literally said in the context of the French Revolution was "An invasion of armies can be resisted; an invasion of ideas cannot be resisted."

Although Salahuddin conquered Jerusalem in a battle of arms, it was ultimately won for humanity by his chivalry, honor, compassion, and justice.

We don't need to rely on Tolkien's "Middle Earth" to artificially motivate us to attain redemption. Salahuddin's universal legacy is sufficient.

Today, we gravitate between fiction and reality in managing our social, political, and spiritual lives. Actuality is fused with "fake news" in a way that crafts a faulty perception of reality. Fiction, though often far-reaching, is no substitute for reality.

Experience teaches us that the more we witness change in a rapidly developing and technologically advanced world, the more it harkens us back to the same timeless moralities of truth, justice, freedom, and peace. Now is the time to act on those principles, which require discipline and mutual engagement.

Otherwise, our country is heading in the wrong direction. However, we can change course because…

Nothing is more powerful than an idea whose time has come.

Islam is a powerful idea and a way of life. Muslims may be a minority in America, but for nearly fifteen hundred years, Islam has stood on its own merits as a civilizational competitor to Western hegemony, and has its own challenges for humanity, calling us to live up to and practice here at home what we preach to the rest of the world abroad.

As a Muslim-American living two vibrant realities, I am a link of sorts bridging a gap of empathy between Islam and America. I sincerely hope this humble effort will lead to a much-needed wider discussion and more understanding.

I love to engage with people, and on the very topics our secular society considers taboo in polite conversation: politics and religion. As a lawyer, I seek to analyze and solve problems for my clients. I realize that the people I converse with are looking for something more than they have in their lives. They are at a disadvantage in engaging with me because I share their common lived experience here in America, with all that it entails, but mostly, they know nothing about Islam and how it harmonizes faith and reason.

I like to think I am convincing them of something, and at times I am. However, what really turns their heads are the exploratory questions and the topics I raise. By challenging conventional wisdom, I am opening eyes and minds to issues that most people don't really give enough thought to in their busy, economically driven American lives.

As a Muslim, I believe faith has a role to play in the free marketplace of ideas, and religion is not obsolete or irrelevant. Muslims believe Islam is the perfect balance between the known and the unknown, faith and reason, and human advancement and the checks and balances to that advancement.

Here are some questions I ask based on my experiences and observations.

Why do we divide our political views from our religious convictions?

Why do we think we simply came into existence from nothing?

Why do some Christians criticize Islam for perceived faults that are actually in Christianity?

Why don't more Americans support the Palestinian cause?

Why does society accept multiple forms of marital unions but reject polygamy?

Why does our openly liberal society absorb itself in "cancel culture" and tend not to forgive?

Why do we hold others to a higher standard on the use of violence than we allow ourselves?

Why do some blame the status of women only on patriarchy?

Why is racism a major problem in America?

Why is food making us sick?

Do we believe in the human ability to rehabilitate?

These are just some of the questions and topics raised in this book. It is a collection of essays connected together by my experiences as a Palestinian, Muslim, and immigrant to the US. The chapters that follow provide a survey of challenging aspects of Islam for America.

And some humble answers along the way.

This book will challenge what you think you know about Islam and Muslims, and the seemingly provocative alternatives offered in it. For example, allowing the families of murder victims to have a greater say in the fate of the killer when clemency is sought can foster forgiveness in society, decrease the murder rate, break the vicious cycle of recidivism in communities of color, and strengthen the ties between the prosecutor's office and the community. This is not a new concept of justice. Islam allows for forgiveness in lieu of the death penalty.

This and other topics are relevant in America today. We seem to have lost our bearings on religion, politics, and society. The government shouldn't be defining marriage for us. US foreign policy on Palestine has to change to reflect a just position on human rights for all. Islam and Muslims are not the source of violence and terror. Injustice and extremism are the catalysts. True feminism combats abuse of power without pitting the sexes against each other. Abstaining from food is not only healthy, it also curbs greed.

Are any of these topics relevant to you?

If you are concerned about your future, this book is for you. If you are a decision-maker, policy-maker, or are in the halls of power, this serves as a reality check of where we are and where we need to go to avoid civil war. Sound advice can come from the most remote quarters, but we have to be willing to accept it nevertheless.

Note of caution: This book will foster in you the courage to be thick-skinned. Those sensitive to criticism, prepare to have your worldview challenged.

How to Read This Book

―

"We are all slaves to something"
—UNKNOWN

I feel empathy and sorrow when I hear prevalent platitudes from people, such as: *I believe in myself. I am spiritual, but I don't believe in religion* or *I believe in God but...* These people can be smart, fiercely independent-minded and overall well-intentioned and decent individuals. Yet, such individuals are burdened by a reality. They are slaves to someone or something in this world.

This book is particularly intended for people of other faiths and no faith at all. For better or worse, America has a long-term relationship with Islam and Muslims. Islam and Muslims are all too often feared, misunderstood, and sometimes ignored. If America is the most influential nation in the world, then Islam is the most influential religion in the world. Whatever your opinions are on the subject, Islam's prevalence has far-reaching consequences for Americans, Muslims, and the world. The issues raised in this book affect you and me. Can you imagine the significance of benefiting from both what America has to offer and what Islam has to offer our society? I am a Muslim-American with an experience to share and a story to tell.

The meanings of the same words can have differing effects depending on who is writing them. You need to know where I am coming from in terms of my worldview and motivations. Otherwise, what I say can be misconstrued as irrelevant and off base, insincere, arrogant, or even dangerous.

I invite you to join me with an open mind.

Keeping an open mind means a willingness to consider new ideas in an unprejudiced way. Engage in this book with the mindset that you are right with the possibility of being wrong, and that I am wrong with the possibility of being right. Keeping an open mind also entails assuming good intentions on the part of the other, unless said person clearly exhibits unequivocal hatred or ill will.

You may be conditioned, by society and the Western emphasis on individualism, to abhor the idea of submitting your will to something else. However, we are all slaves to something. Think for a moment. What, on a basic level, motivates you, informs your disposition, and drives you to pursue your desires in life? Your will can be as lofty as dedicating your life to a faith-based purpose or as base as succumbing to a vicious cycle of bad habits. In this way, we are all subjugated to something, whether it be status, wealth, greed, material possessions, eating disorders, deviant sexual behavior, or other people, such as celebrities and their influences.

At the same time, we are all born with an innate knowledge of a greater being than ourselves who is one and indivisible. Our environment, upbringing, and society deviates us for a period of time from appreciating and recognizing this initial disposition of ours. It's not acceptable to surrender our will without exercising our intellects to search for truth and meaning.

For me, Islam offers freedom through submission. By freely choosing to submit my will to God, I liberate myself, mentally and spiritually, from the confinements of this worldly life to the expansiveness of a continued existence after bodily death. I am not a slave to other fallible human beings like me, but a worshipper of the Lord of all human beings.

It was not always like that for me, though. Growing up, not only did I question the existence of God, but as a child I converted to Christianity and accepted Jesus Christ as my Lord and Savior. I also studied and looked into other major faiths of the world before I eventually reverted to Islam, the faith all people are born into. My journey is not unique. We all search for something throughout our lives. My search led me to some conclusions that will aid you in understanding the motivations and reasoning behind some of the issues presented in this book and the manner in which I raise them.

Some will say this book is an invitation to embrace Islam. To a certain extent, I have an obligation to call people to what I believe is the ultimate truth. It is more than that, though. If you don't settle upon your own truth or it is not inclusive enough or relevant enough to propagate to others, know that people are out there with their own vision to which they call others to embrace. Muslims pray five times a day with open eyes, literally. The point being, worship is not intended to seclude one from the world, along with its ups and downs, but rather fuse faith, reason, and action in harmony. For Muslims, our lives are not compartmentalized into the sacred and the profane. This means we don't have to experience a disconnect between politics and religion, personal and public life, or between life and death.

A market-driven society like ours thrives on distorting reality to create alternative perceptions of it. Outwardly, we're the envy of much of the world, commercializing everything is appealing and generates profits. However, the long-term effects of this habitual practice can be negative and debilitating. Look at unrealistic depictions of beauty, body types, life styles, and careers, and the negative effects such a facade has on the consumer. Perception can be powerful, but it does not replace reality. The reality of Islam is a gift in the free marketplace of ideas.

Christianity, with over two billion adherents, and other religions are a force to be reckoned with regardless of whether one believes in them or not. Islam has been a source of guidance and its ideological reach comprehensively competes with any Western ideology or religion on Earth. The staying power of the *Qur'an* is self-evident. If you were to read the *Qur'an*, even omitting its many references to God, the reality of its uprightness, wisdom, and approach would still be a model for human existence because it challenges human beings to think, ponder, and question their dispositions and surroundings. At the same time, it empowers us to act with dignity, fortitude, and morality. It recognizes our weaknesses and allows us to build on our potential. Islam is not merely a religion but a comprehensive way of life in harmony with reality.

In theory, all people should be understood according to their professed beliefs, and they should be held accountable for their actions by objective universal standards of goodness, decency, and fairness. As Americans, we are understood by others based on our preachings of liberalism, democracy, freedom, individualism, and economic prosperity. Islam and Muslims challenge us to be true to our own ideas of what it means to be an American, and the ideals we profess about ourselves and to the world.

We are judged, though, on whether we justifiably bomb other countries, jail our own citizens, or shun others who do not look or speak like us. If we consider our life the best way of life, we have to be prepared to act on our beliefs, lead by example, and tangibly show a net positive contribution to the world beyond economic prosperity.

Muslims should be understood based on the sources of their faith, i.e., the *Qur'an* and example of the Prophet Muhammad. We have to let the *Qur'an* speak for itself, and we have to learn how Muslims view their prophet. Muslims consider themselves the best group of people if their actions promote what's good and prevent what's bad while believing in God. Keep in mind that Muslims are not a race, ethnicity, nationality, or linguistic community. The most unlikely candidate today can become a Muslim tomorrow. As a goal of this book, hopefully, I will be able to effectively articulate some Islamic concepts and rationales of value for an audience conditioned to divide church and state, or where religion does not inform one's worldview.

Muslims should be judged based on their actions in enjoining good and preventing evil, and whether they justifiably bomb other countries, jail their own citizens, or shun others who are different. In this assessment-based approach, religious people are on an equal footing with everyone else. I differentiate between rejecting immoral behavior based on my religious beliefs and accepting the need for an equal protection of the law and due process to all people living under the rule of law. I can't demand rights for my religion, using the law as a justification, and then turn around and deny someone else's rights by the same rationale. As a Muslim, there are behaviors and actions I dislike, but my religion tells me that I cannot discriminate in legal terms against a person just because I oppose their behavior.

What truly distinguishes us is the overall good we can do for ourselves and others to alleviate human suffering, such as disease, abject poverty, mental anguish, unjustified violence, and war. Those are worthy causes for which we can engage ourselves in mutual competition. Those who decide to run for office or are appointed to positions of power and influence have an added obligation to competently fulfill their obligations fairly and honestly as they serve those over whom they rule. As Americans, we like to think we are the freest people on the earth. We are ruled over, though, by those who don't govern or set policy in alignment with our issues. How free are we then?

As great as our country is, with its innovative democratic experience, it still manages to produce some of the least moral, honest, and dignified presidents and candidates for office we have seen in the past couple of generations. Why would we let someone who is less honest, fair, moral, and concerned about humanity than we are lead us? That is folly. Major religions insist on this higher standard of morality and ethics we expect from our elected leaders.

One common criticism of Islam is that it is resistant to change. In a technologically advanced liberal society, Islam is viewed as backward. In reality, it is consistent and anchors us to timeless virtues. While religion in the West is receding, Islam is the world's fastest growing religion (Pew Research). While vested interests only attribute such growth to birth rates, it downplays conversion, especially in the West. This consistency in continuity of faith, history, morality, and shared cultural ethics allows a new Muslim convert to tap into a rich Islamic history that spans fourteen hundred years and the globe.

This is depth.

Omar Ibn Al Khattab, the second Caliph or leader of the early Muslim community, was known for his ethics, morality, justice, and piety. Under his leadership, two empires crumbled beneath his feet, yet he was still and first a humble servant of God. Once a former Persian governor was brought to Medina, the capital of the empire at the time. The once high-ranking official was directed to a public area near the mosque where he found Ibn al Khattab sleeping in midday (Qailula in Arabic and siesta in Spanish). He marveled at this sight and commented, "O' Prince of the Believers, because you governed with justice, you felt secure in your heart, and therefore you slept."

Today, to those of us with power and privilege, I ask, do we hold ourselves accountable before we are held accountable for our decisions and actions? It is no mistake that the authors of the preamble to the Constitution purposefully predicated domestic tranquility (today, it is what we call national security) on the establishment of justice. Two hundred and thirty years ago, the word "justice," which is derived from the Latin meaning law, was founded in part upon God's law. In religion lies morality. While the meaning of justice has become relative and changed over time, it behooves us to go back to a simple concept to help us understand the immutability of justice as the absence of oppression in all things.

I use the word "God" throughout this book because it is the familiar English term for the concept of the Supreme Being and Creator. In Arabic, the language of the *Qur'an* (God's speech to us), the proper name of God is "Allah." Allah is referred to as "He" because Arabic pronoun usage does not include the neutral gender "it" and is limited to feminine and masculine references. Unlike in English, though, where "god" can be made into "goddess," the word "Allah" is neither male nor female. Nor can the word "Allah" be pluralized into "gods," for example. The etymology of the term "Allah" is similar in other Semitic languages such as Aramaic and Hebrew. Allah is also the word Christian Arabs use to refer to God in the *Bible*.

Keep in mind that any reference to Jesus, Moses, Muhammad, or any of the prophets, while not written, invokes the prayer "God's peace and blessings upon him."

My faith tells me if I have a proclivity toward certain unhealthy desires, it doesn't mean I have to act upon them. Innate human dignity tells us that being happy does not mean following one's desires wherever they lead without limit, just as long as it isn't illegal.

I have done my best to avoid unnecessary criticism of people, institutions, and other beliefs. Due to my collective experiences in witnessing injustice, hatred, and racist bigotry, my emotions may at times interject. What is good and of use in this book I attribute to God, and what is lacking or negative, I take responsibility for.

Everyone is a slave to something. That is why I choose to be a slave to the Unseen, Omnipotent all Merciful God so that I am not a slave to other human beings, their worldviews, material things, status, or anything of this world. That's what makes me free to write this book even if it's not popular. The Constitution gives me the freedom of speech to do so, but the right to free speech is only as good as how we utilize it for good. Once I have submitted my human will to God, I can be free to do what is good for humankind without being fettered by other constraints. These are my beliefs and my way of life, and this is my approach to writing this book.

What I ask from you is to read these pages with an open mind and heart. Take in what I am saying before you form your opinion, and allow the possibility for your beliefs or ideas about Islam and Muslims to be changed.

CHAPTER 1

It Does Me No Injury

"It does me no injury for my neighbor to say there are twenty gods or no God. It neither picks my pocket nor breaks my leg."
—THOMAS JEFFERSON

One of the hallmarks of the American contribution to the democratic experience is freedom of religion. In theory, it did not matter to Jefferson and the founding fathers what one's religious beliefs, or lack thereof, were as long as no legal harm came from it. This worked relatively well when the burgeoning United States consisted of mostly protestant Christian denominations and a vocal deist intelligentsia. Fast-forward two and a half centuries later, this beacon of religious freedom is losing its bearings. Religion is declining in America. Yet, it still plays a vital role in the lives of millions of Americans. Mostly a "Christian nation," America has witnessed the rise of Islam—a religion that erases the barrier between religion and state. What the American secular state accepts for itself, e.g., the justification to make war on other nations, it does not afford to others.

Many critics of Islam fault the Prophet Muhammad for his participation in war, something the United States has been engaged in nonstop for over a century, not to mention the colonizers use of Christianity against indigenous populations. However, in the conquest of Mecca, the Prophet Muhammad did not kill the vanquished. He spared their lives—a remarkable feat at the time as it went against the norm.

When the Prophet seized the city, he famously said to the inhabitants, "O Quraish, what do you think of the treatment that I should accord you?"

And they said, "Mercy, O Prophet of God. We expect nothing but good from you."

Thereupon, Muhammad declared, "I speak to you in the same words as Joseph spoke to his brothers. This day there is no reproof against you; Go your way, for you are free."

Muhammad's stature grew in all of Arabia after the surrender of the Meccans. Delegates from all over the peninsula came to Medina to accept his suzerainty and prophethood.

The Islamic empire was born.

At first glance, Christianity appears to be a religion of love, mercy, and forgiveness while Islam is viewed as a political movement disguised in religious garb characterized by rigid laws and a transactional, deed-based creed as a means of salvation. The perception of some is that in Islam one enters paradise based on one's deeds, while Christians enter heaven based on God's mercy in the form of accepting Jesus Christ as one's Lord and Savior.

Jefferson and the Founding Fathers were a product of their times. As descendants of European immigrants to the "new land," they were averse to a Catholic church governing both secular and religious affairs. European monarchs had incrementally established their secular authority at the expense of the Church in Western Christendom.

The United States would be that "City upon a hill" exhibiting the best of Western democracy and moral life. One of the main pillars to achieve such a vision was dividing church and state.

So how does this "Christian" nation deal with criminal sanctions like the death penalty and life imprisonment? Is the criminal justice system conducive to rehabilitation?

CRIME AND PUNISHMENT
In Islam, the punishment for stealing is to have one's hand cut off. Admittedly, the concept immediately strikes us as barbaric and backward. In addition to the harm that theft brings to society as Jefferson alluded to, the enactment of punishment on the perpetrator comes with its own harms. The thief is jailed, fined, and humiliated. Most would agree that one deserves such a punishment for the crime of theft. What happens, though, when the punishment causes harm that outweighs the crime?

In Thailand, a man was sentenced to 141,078 years for a financial crime. Even in the US, Sholam Weiss was sentenced to 845 years for bankrupting a life insurance company. Bernard Madoff, who died in prison this year, was sentenced to 159 years for a Ponzi scheme.

Now, ask yourself: would you rather spend the rest of your life in prison or have your hand cut off?

Which punishment is a more effective deterrent? Which punishment allows for rehabilitation? Which punishment leads to more overall harm to society?

In Islamic law, the penalty of cutting the hand for stealing is the deterrent. The carrying out of the sentence is the rehabilitation. Communal shaming can be an effective way of bringing down the crime rate. Muslim scholars agree that a prosthetic hand to replace the severed limb is a mercy from God that allows the rehabilitated person to gain back some use of his or her hand while living with the stigma of having committed a crime. Regardless, the person is able to be reassimilated into society as a rehabilitated individual.

In 1994–95, while a law student at Indiana University-Bloomington, I volunteered as a prisoner rights advocate as part of the law school's student legal clinic. In this capacity, I met Nidal Ayyad, a man who had been sentenced to 240 years in prison for his role in the 1993 World Trade Center bombing.

As a member of a Judeo-Christian-Islamic tradition, fellow practicing Jews and Christians and I believe that Adam, Noah, and some other figures in the *Bible* and the *Qur'an* lived for hundreds of years. In the case of the Prophet Noah, nearly a thousand years. Yet, studying law in the greatest country in the world, how is it that such a rational secular society can sentence a person to nearly two-and-a-half centuries when no one currently expects a person to live beyond a third of that age on average? If you contend that religion produces unsubstantiated beliefs, then take note that the creative secular mind also has led to some bizarre outcomes that don't seem to be rational.

Let's examine capital punishment and incarceration in the criminal justice system.

THE DEATH PENALTY

The Prophet Muhammad experienced an incident in his life. As the secular and religious leader of the community, he was approached by a woman of the Ghamidi tribe who came to him and said, "I have committed adultery. I want to be purified of my sin." This meant she was submitting herself to death by stoning. The Prophet turned his face away from her.

She came to him again on the following day. Again, he turned away from her. This time, she told him she was pregnant.

He said, "Come back after you give birth to the child."

She came back months later after giving birth seeking punishment.

He said, "Come back after your child is in no need of suckling."

After two years, she came back with the toddler holding a piece of bread in his hand as evidence that he had been weaned. Only then did the Prophet order her to be stoned.

Even though she self-confessed, he turned her away in an attempt to dissuade her from seeking the penalty. In one of the epilogues to the narration, a companion cursed her for her adultery. The Prophet was upset and rebuked him saying that her repentance was so sincere that it would have sufficed to cleanse the sins of the city.

In the US, both in the federal system and in most states, the decision of whether to seek the death penalty rests with the governing authority. This power is understandable in cases where the harm is widespread or directly affects the sovereignty of the state, such as in mass murders, treason, or armed insurrection. However, most cases involving death row inmates arise locally from the murder of individuals in crimes of passion, rape, armed robbery, and other drug-related offenses, and in some cases, there is a familial or known relationship between the killer and the victim(s).

For a nation that prides itself on the development of its progress toward a more humane and civilized society, it is cynical that the government prosecution routinely ignores the wishes of the families of the victims in cases where they forgive the killer or explicitly request clemency for the murderer. In addition, inhumanely long sentences are routinely applied, undermining the opportunity for rehabilitation. Religious principles can play a positive role in these situations.

Islamic law is criticized for allowing capital punishment. Yet, at least in the case of murder, there is commonality. It is sanctioned by Islam, here in America, and in the majority of the states. Even though there is a worldwide trend toward abolishing capital punishment, there is no empirical evidence that doing so directly diminishes the number of deaths caused by human beings through murder, war, or political repression. Worldwide, a homicide takes place nearly every minute of the day. If we take into consideration the deaths caused annually by war, one innocent life is lost every several seconds.

BY SANITIZING DEATH, WE CAUSE MORE OF IT

The death penalty as a deterrent in Islam is highly dependent on a public exhibition of the sentence being carried out. For the most part in the US, unless it's of national notoriety, the only time we hear of convicts being put to death is in newspapers and local news. Even then, we are not shown the excruciating and final death throes of the person being put to death. In this hushed-up manner, the state's case for deterrence is weakened. Capital punishment as a deterrent would be more effective if it was publicized and a meaningful portion of society was required to see it personally and up close. This publicizing of death (as a means of decreasing overall death) is not limited to the death penalty. It applies to other causes of death, such as war.

Nearly three thousand innocent civilians died in the 9/11 attacks. Since 9/11, more than seven thousand of our men and women in uniform have died (this number does not include the over seven thousand government contractor deaths in Afghanistan and Iraq in the past eighteen years or so) and been brought back in body bags, but the Pentagon only allows journalists to show us the rows of coffins, if the family permits it. This has only been the policy for a little over a decade. Previously, there was an eighteen-year ban on such photos.

From an Islamic perspective, the wisdom behind public displays of death is to elicit an aversion for engaging in those actions of murder and unjust war that cause pain, death, and destruction. In a secular society where religion is no longer relied upon to explain death, evil, and the unknown, we tend to desensitize ourselves to death by ignoring and capsulizing it into a soundbite or a button on a screen, as in the case of precision technology drones where one can kill wholesale while sitting down at a table and drinking coffee. Furthermore, there is the added problem of disconnecting the action of, say, pressing a button while looking at a screen, and the actual gory results of such action. This lack of answers for the unknown may explain our attraction to horror movies, science fiction, and Hollywood thrillers. We like to become artificially scared from a movie because it gives us control over what we created, yet it's a false sense of security.

LONG PRISON SENTENCES ARE NOT ALWAYS THE ANSWER
Islam is more retrospective when it comes to safeguarding life, liberty, and property. Therefore, short of the death penalty, even a life sentence, when the full ramifications of such a punishment are considered, is problematic. Yes, the person is not put to death. Yes, the person, in most instances, is allowed to breathe, eat, drink, sleep, smoke, workout, read,

write, play an instrument, pray, meditate, opine, think, and partake in other activities and faculties of the mind. However, the long-term deprivation of freedom of the human being in confinement can be worse than death for some. Some, maybe most human beings, would prefer life in prison over death. For the significant numbers of others who cannot fathom the thought of having their freedom taken away from them permanently, minute after minute, hour after hour, day after day, week after week, month after month, year after year, death would be preferable to the horror of mental anguish, depression, and/or the insanity a state of mind can reach.

In Islamic law, imprisonment is sanctioned. However, unlike US law where it is rudimentary, punitive detention was considered supplementary to enforcing corporal punishments such as *hudud* and *t'azir*. In other words, Islamic law allowed for other forms of punishment like flogging, severance of the hand, and other public displays of shaming. Long prison sentences were viewed as tyrannical and associated with the oppressive whim of the sovereign in punishing political dissent. The rationale was that God created man to be free, and it was not within the jurisdiction of the state to curtail such freedom in this drastic manner. One may instinctively consider flogging and cutting of limbs as backward and barbaric. However, depriving a human being of liberty for life can be a much more cruel and unusual punishment.

In the case of Nidal Ayyad, I went to visit him after he wrote to our clinic complaining of his treatment, and my professor thought I would be the best intern for the task. Mr. Ayyad was being mistreated in prison. He was abused physically and verbally. His privileges were taken away without due process, and he felt dehumanized. Although he maintained his innocence, he felt his role in the bombing was exploited for political motives by the prosecution, at the time he preferred death over a 240-year sentence. Six people had died, and thousands were injured as a result of the bombing. Except for the purpose of making him suffer more by keeping him confined for life, why wouldn't the law allow for a self-imposed death penalty?

A pettiness, I recall, of some prison officials was that after my initial intake visit, I was denied a second visit. In a writing to my professor at the clinic, the Bureau of Prisons cited security reasons for denying me visitation with Nidal. The warden said the guards noticed that Nidal and I resembled each other and insinuated that would pose a risk of escape.

All such visits were constantly monitored by prison guards. There were some "scary" features we had in common; we were about the same age, but he was about half a foot taller and outweighed me by about twenty to thirty pounds, we were both of Arab origin, we both wore glasses, and most important of all, we both kept beards. The "resemblance" was "uncanny." Honestly, I would have preferred the warden to just say all Arabs look alike. I would have been less offended than the feigned security threat that I posed to the prison in visiting my client. Suffice it to say, the BOP backed down by a mere threat to sue, and I was able to visit Nidal again to help with his grievances.

The political retribution for Nidal's alleged role in the bombing was palpable both in the overkill sentence of 240 years and the discrimination he faced as a convicted "terrorist."

Such vindictiveness of a democratic state that claims to be morally superior exposed a double standard. And, cruelty in life sentences has its precedents. Given the historical prevalence of capital punishment throughout all civilizations and its current reality around the world and in the US, I am not making an argument for its complete abolition. We will deal with the world as it is.

MERCY AND FORGIVENESS SHOULD BE PART OF THE PENAL CODE

In Islamic law, there is the concept of forgiveness or monetary compensation for the family of the deceased in lieu of execution. The closest of kin can opt for the death penalty, compensation, or forgiveness of the perpetrator. In the American context of harmonizing church and state, we can benefit from this concept of justice. Notwithstanding the deterrence interest of the state, it makes sense that the most affected in the aftermath of the murder should have the most say in the matter.

Ironically, in the American penal system where the death penalty is codified and at least some punishment involving the deprivation of freedom is mandatory. There is no allowance, from the outset, for clemency. Whereas in Islam, the practice of mercy is embedded in the system. In such cases, this does not only mean (for the offender) the avoidance of death but potentially averting a prison sentence as well, or at least one significantly less than life in prison. It can bring down the crime rate by curtailing recidivism. This can have a transformational effect on the criminal justice system in terms of reforming local communities after serious crimes; case in point: Lexington, Kentucky, 2015.

On April 19, 2015 at about 3:00 a.m. in Lexington, Kentucky, a young man was murdered. One of the killers was Trey Alexander Relford. Salahuddin Ayyub Jitmoud was twenty-two years old when he was stabbed and his throat was slit in a robbery while delivering pizza. As a mere statistic, he was one of approximately 15,695 people murdered in the US that year.

His father, Abdul-Munim Sombat Jitmoud, described Salahuddin as modest, hardworking, and dedicated to his faith. Noteworthy, there was an incident that the father relates about his son in light of the recent UPS policy allowing drivers to keep beards in an effort "to celebrate diversity rather than corporate restrictions."

Salahuddin worked in a distribution center at UPS. He did such a good job that he was offered a promotion to a delivery driver. However, in compliance with UPS's personal appearance policy at the time, it was conditioned on him shaving off his beard. Because he kept a beard for religious reasons, he couldn't move up the corporate ladder and went back to stacking boxes. Had the UPS policy been more accommodating at the time, his destiny may have been different.

What made this otherwise mundane murder case truly something special was the victim impact statement of Salahuddin's father and what he did afterward.

Mr. Jitmoud is a US citizen and Muslim immigrant from Thailand. He and his wife, who passed away a couple of years before Salahuddin's murder, raised six boys together. He is soft spoken, of humble beginnings, hailing from the rice fields and farmland of a small village in Thailand. He earned his PhD in the US in education and worked as an educator and principal at various schools for children.

In his victim impact statement, he focused his calming gaze and attention on the killer, Trey Alexander Relford, a young African American man only a couple of years older than Salahuddin at the time of his death. The grief-struck father said, "My dear Trey, I don't blame you for the crime you have committed. I am not angry at you… I am angry at the devil; I blame the devil," a mesmerized audience gazed at him as he gently continued, "who misguided you and who misled you to do such a horrible crime."

He expressed sorrow for his parents because they raised Trey and wanted him to be successful. As an educator he elaborated, "Your success is their success. Your happiness is their happiness. Now they have to cry because of the crime you committed."

His fatherly instincts kicked in as he said, "My son, my nephew, I forgive you on behalf of Salahuddin and his mother." Acknowledging those present in the courtroom with a glance, he told Trey, "Forgiveness is the greatest gift of charity in Islam."

After this extraordinary outpouring of compassion, a teary-eyed judge thanked him and ordered a recess. Upon commencement of the proceedings, Trey's allocution was similarly heartfelt. He acknowledged his guilt and expressed remorse, thanked his victim's father for his kindness, and applauded him as a "powerful man" to be as hurt as he was yet get up there and say what he said.

In addressing the father, who was positioned behind him and to his right, Trey was overwhelmed and began to sob using the collar of his orange jumpsuit to wipe away the tears. Mr. Jitmoud, edging closer as he was being addressed, extended his hand to offer a tissue. When Trey reached out to take it, the retired principal latched on to his hand and pulled Trey tightly to his bosom in a warm embrace, so wholesome it could not even be tainted by the "bar" partition between them, plunging the courtroom into audible sounds of unrestrained sobbing.

Salahuddin's father later commented that he wanted to forgive Trey to open the way for him to be forgiven by God and embark on a new, better life. In Islam, repentance is complete, in situations where a fellow human being was wronged, when forgiveness is also sought of the wronged party.

Salahuddin's father's huge act of compassion was acknowledged by all involved. The police chief praised him not only as a community leader, but a role model who forged a path for others to follow with his forgiveness.

Even though the white judge was moved by this extraordinary display of humanity, it did not prompt her to lighten Trey's sentence. He pled guilty, instead of going to trial, to avoid the death penalty. She accepted the Commonwealth's recommendation of thirty-one years and sentenced him accordingly. The impression lingers that people of color disproportionately receive higher sentences than whites in similar situations, thus weakening the proportionality and deterrence factors.

In a similar vein, we apply extreme sentences to parents who harm their own children, almost as if trying to one-up the damage they've done to themselves with such an action. In Texas, a twenty-three-year-old Hispanic woman, Elizabeth Escalona, was sentenced to ninety-nine years in prison for viciously beating her two-year-old daughter into a coma. The law allowed for a sentence anywhere from probation to ninety-nine years. The prosecution initially sought a forty-five-year sentence and then upped it to ninety-nine years. She received this sentence despite evidence presented by the defense of effective psychological counseling leading to rehabilitation and a letter pleading for mercy from one of her other children and family support testimony.

The system has a false sense of righteousness embedded into it. The judge was an older white gentleman who belied his ostensible motive of judging this woman, who herself was a victim of sexual abuse, under the pretext of protecting the innocent child. However, he showed no mercy for the perpetrator despite the family support she clearly had. And the prosecutor who justified seeking a ninety-year sentence stating that the mother did not show adequate remorse, goes home to her family apparently oblivious to the harm she has caused not only to the mother but the entire extended family, especially the children. What about the little girl? It's one thing to keep her away from her abusive mother, which is a good thing; however, to grow up with an incarcerated mother has its own set of harms and challenges. The life sentence will ensure the child relives the abuse in an additional way for the rest of her life.

Islamic law, rich in a body of tradition and precedent, recognizes a difference between harm of parent to child versus harm of child to parent. In some schools of Islamic jurisprudence, a man cannot be put to death for killing his child, whereas a son can be put to death for killing his father. The rationale for such a dichotomy is simple but rational. The child literally emanated from his parents, therefore, is not entirely independent of them. It would be the epitome of depravity, arrogance, betrayal, and ungratefulness to take that life, regardless of abuse. The child, other than ultimately to God, owes his or her existence to the parents. The child can permanently sever ties with the parents without having to mete out vengeance.

On the other hand, if a parent descends to such a level of rage to the point of killing his own child, no death sentence or prison sentence outweighs the self-harm committed. Would we sentence a person to life imprisonment for attempting to take one's own life? Killing one's own child or beating them is like inflicting that act upon oneself because a child is literally a physical part of oneself. In most cases, that is punishment enough without having the state interfere in domestic affairs to create more anguish, pain, and orphaned children.

This is not to say there should be no punishment for these crimes, rather determining the most appropriate punishment under the circumstances, and in a way that best leads to rehabilitation and comports with human dignity.

Elizabeth Escalona needed counseling, family support, and a monitoring system. Other family members could have taken over custody of the child. The state has no right to destroy an entire family, especially the victim in this case, under some guise of protecting that innocent child. Did these same Americans who claim to be fighting for child victims care about the denial of DACA benefits for youth who came as young children and those separated from their parents, and placed in cages, on the Texas-Mexican border?

Harm is relative, and the harm caused to people of color and minorities is given less weight. It would not matter if white defendants were treated the same in similar circumstances, it would still be wrong. This is not an issue of race. It is an issue of fairness, justice, and discharging a public trust for those who rule over us and claim to represent our interests. What we perceive as backwardness and a greater harm, can actually be a better method of comporting dignity to human beings and rehabilitating those who, due to the disparity of justice in society, fall to crime.

Islamic law is patterned on a different methodology and legislated under strict rules of morality while educating and encouraging society to behave modestly. If someone falls from grace, the spirit of the law finds ways to make up for those faults. This encourages the dignity and self-worth of human beings rather than driving people into despair as unworthy or hopeless.

In another prophetic story, a young man approached the Prophet Muhammad in the company of others and asked for permission to commit adultery. Those gathered around rebuked him for his audacity. The Prophet drew him near and sat him down.

"Would you like that for your mother?" he asked the young man.

Embarrassed, the youth replied no and exalted the Prophet.

"Neither would people like it for their mothers. Would you like that for your daughter?"

He replied no, and again lauded the Prophet by offering himself as a sacrifice.

The Prophet said, "Neither would people like it for their daughters. Would you like that for your sister?"

"No," came the reply.

"Neither would people like it for their sisters. Would you like that for your aunts?"

The man said, "No, by God, may I be a ransom for you."

The Prophet said, "Neither would people like it for their aunts."

Then, the Prophet placed his hand on the young man and said, "O' God, forgive his sins, purify his heart, and guard his chastity."

After that, the young man never again inclined to such sinful behavior.

In 1972, the California Supreme Court held the death penalty unconstitutional on the grounds that it constituted cruel and unusual punishment. Based on that decision, Sirhan Sirhan, a Christian Palestinian, the convicted killer of Robert F. Kennedy, had his death sentence commuted to life in prison with the possibility of parole. Since then, he has attended sixteen parole hearings, the last one was in 2021.

At one of the hearings, a Kennedy confidant, Paul Schrade, who was shot walking behind Kennedy, pleaded for Sirhan's release. He forgave him and apologized for not working earlier on his release.

"I forgive you for shooting me," Schrade told Sirhan. "I should have been here long ago and that's why I feel guilty for not being here to help you and to help me." Schrade was ninety-one at the time.

After visiting his father's convicted killer in 2017, Robert F. Kennedy, Jr. said he supported the call for a reinvestigation of the assassination. He didn't believe Sirhan acted alone or was necessarily responsible for his father's death. In spite of the sentiment of forgiveness of those directly impacted by the events of 1968, and the state parole board of California granting Sirhan parole, his freedom is in limbo with the state's governor. He has been in prison for over a half century. He is now seventy-seven years old.

The Kennedy assassinations have had a profound impact on our nation. It stands to reason that the state apparatus has a vested interest in the outcome of such a politically charged event as the killing of Robert F. Kennedy. However, it also has a sacred trust, that is, to dispense justice.

Since no reinvestigation is forthcoming and he meets the qualifications under California law, why shouldn't he be released?

Death of human beings at the hands of other human beings is inevitable. However, it can be diminished overall through spiritual education and state-applied death penalty only in the most grievous cases. And even then, family-member forgiveness should be taken into consideration.

CHAPTER 2

Let Them Marry

A polygamist was prohibited by US immigration laws from bringing his second wife to America.

The immigration officer said, "According to our laws, polygamy makes her inadmissible. Your petition is denied." (Foreign Affairs Manual)

The polygamist rebutted, "But you allow gay men and women to bring their spouses." (Foreign Affairs Manual)

The immigration officer's tone became sterner, "In a free society like ours, we allow consenting adults to benefit from the same rights heterosexual married couples enjoy."

Becoming hopeful, the polygamist said, "I know I am twenty-two years older than my second wife, but we were married on her eighteenth birthday, so she consented."

The immigration officer condescendingly responded, "Look, sir, you can either divorce your wife or appeal my decision."

Stroking his beard several times, the polygamist finally said, "The Islamic Republic of Iran has been recognizing transgender individuals since I was born, and it performs more sex change operations than any other nation in the world except Thailand (US Citizenship and Immigration Services). I'll have her operated on and bring 'him' as my husband. Howdya like dem apples?"

Eying him squarely, the immigration officer, with a smirk on his face, responded, "Go ahead, the president just signed an executive order banning all males from Iran."

Defiant, the polygamist said, "I am not moving until I am reunited with both of my wives." Seeing his frustration, the immigration officer said, "Look, buddy, we don't allow polygamy. It goes against the morality of the country." (Barford)

Frustrated, he said "Can I ask you a question? I've had a relationship with two women in my life. How many women have you had a relationship with?" The officer raised his eyebrows and said nothing.

As the dejected man walked away, the officer who had been counting on his fingers called back at him, "Hey, buddy, about fifteen or sixteen."

This is a joke, but it is reflective of the current state of disparity in how our laws treat different types of consenting adult relationships and their rights under US law.

Gallup Poll has been tracking American attitudes on morality. The surprising trend is on polygamy. When Gallup first included polygamy on the list in 2003, 7 percent of Americans said it was morally acceptable, and that fell to 5 percent in 2006. Over the past decade, this percentage has gradually increased—moving into double digits in 2011, reaching 16 percent in 2015, and this year, at 20 percent, the highest in our history. In short, there has been a fourfold increase in the American public's acceptance of polygamy in about a decade and a half (Newport).

Polygamy ranks high in the criticisms of Islam in the West. Polygamy itself is widely misunderstood, even by Muslims. Its mainstream practice in Islam is undeservedly regarded as immoral and/or anti-feminist. However, the case for the practice of Islamic polygamy is a powerful and rational one on many levels, even in our times.

US laws banning polygamy date back over a century and a half and are ongoing (Vile). Today, given the constitutional legitimization of same sex marriages, due process, and equal protection of the laws will ultimately have to include polygamy. The rationale that recognized gay marriages, that of marital rights for consenting adults, certainly applies to polygamy. Until recently, while immigration laws barring polygamy have been in effect, same sex marriage was unheard of, yet polygamy, rooted in religious belief, also involves consenting adults seeking benefits accessible to other married couples (Guillen).

What is polygamy? Polygamy is the practice or custom of having more than one wife or husband at the same time. The practice of a man having more than one wife is called *polygyny*. The practice of a woman having more than one husband is known as *polyandry*. *Polyamory* is the practice of engaging in multiple, usually sexual, relationships with the consent of all the people involved and doesn't necessarily involve marriage. For the sake of familiarity, I will use polygyny and polygamy interchangeably. Islam allows polygyny but prohibits polyandry and polyamory. Some feminists view polygyny as exploitive of women, relegating them to a status inferior to men. Liberalism similarly considers Muslim polygamists misogynistic, therefore, lacking in good moral character.

Despite the increasing global population, future threats to human existence remain unknown. Strictly as a matter of procreation, polygyny is by far more effective than polyandry. In terms of proliferating the human species, polygyny has the potential to lead to multiple pregnancies, whereas polyandry can ultimately only lead to one at a time.

Furthermore, polyandry is not common and has never been the norm. In traditional societies, only .47 percent of people practice polyandry while 83.39 percent of them practice polygyny. Only 16.14 percent practice monogamy (Hagan). And of that minute minority that practice polyandry, those societies overwhelmingly engage in what anthropologists call *fraternal polyandry*. This form of polyandry involves a group of brothers sharing the same wife. It has the benefit of keeping inherited wealth in the family. In addition, the male siblings have an incentive to accept, financially support, and rear the child as a nephew or niece, if not as a biological child.

As a general rule, and while both men and women have similar sex drives, men are more readily disposed to arousal than women (van Anders). Sexual arousal for men is less predicated in emotional considerations. (Castleman) (Sine). In addition, men are generally more sexually active, and capable of procreation, in older age than women. Furthermore, many women curtail sexual activity during their menstrual cycle and pregnancy. These are some physiological factors that tend to lend themselves to a proclivity for polygyny.

An added factor with the advent of feminism is the resentment of some men having to compete with women in societal roles traditionally occupied by men. As more and more women enter the workforce, less of their attention is allocated to their traditional family roles. This has led some men to seek female companionship outside the monogamous relationship. And it's not so much the fact that both spouses work, which has become an economic necessity for some, rather it's the attitudes that come along with women's "liberation." A friend of mine once told me, "I didn't marry my wife to compete with her." He voiced a common sentiment among some men whose marriages succeed when there is a delineation of roles within the relationship.

Over the past sixty years, more so than in the past, the average American male engages in *serial monogamy*, which is a form of monogamy characterized by several successive, short-term marriages over the course of a lifetime. For others, while they are monogamous in their sexual relationships, they may not necessarily be married. For example, a Muslim man may have had only two wives simultaneously throughout his life, while his Western counterpart may have had a series of monogamous relationships with dozens of women throughout his life span. This is not to mention those males who may not be faithful to their wives or those who are not married and engaging in sexual relations with more than one woman at a time. This tends to support the rationality of polygamy if fidelity in marriage is an important consideration. However, is man polygamous by nature?

Through DNA analysis, origins of the human species indicate the prevalence of polygyny. Some anthropologists postulate that probably until ten thousand years ago, a few men had a greater effect on the gene pool indicating polygyny (Burchell). Through the tracking of chromosomes, the studies indicate more women were producing than men, and less men were needed to impregnate more women (Hammer) (Labuda). This takes into consideration the fact that women outnumbered men. However, that was not the whole story. It further indicated that less men were contributing to the gene pool because less of them could afford to support many "wives," and more women were traveling with their mates than men leaving their localities. This lends credibility to the theory that men are polygamous by nature.

From a religious perspective, the views on polygamy are varied. Hinduism and Buddhism do not prohibit polygamy, even though it may not be favored. In the Judeo-Christian tradition, the prophets were known to be polygamous. The Torah does not outlaw polygamy. Some Judaic jurists later outlawed polygamy. In Christianity, while there is no direct scriptural prohibition against it, it is generally frowned upon and considered unlawful. Despite this, polygamy existed throughout history in some form to some degree. In my opinion, imposing monogamy leads to unfaithfulness.

C. Owen Lovejoy of Kent State University has hypothesized that "concealed estrus serves to encourage long-term pair-bonding (monogamy) among our male and female ancestors because concealed estrus also conceals the identity of the father of any offspring. Forming a strong bond with a female increases a male's chance that any offspring are his and those offspring are then worth caring for, by providing food, parental care, or other benefits. It is easy to imagine that a strong pair-bond improves the survival of the offspring" (Schacht). Are infidelity and sexual deviances, therefore, the price we pay for our fragile form of monogamy?

Islamic jurisprudence limits polygamy and regulates its practice according to moral principles. When Islam appeared in the mid-seventh century, polygamy historically had no limitations on the number of wives a man was allowed to marry. The Prophet Solomon was said to have three hundred wives and seven hundred concubines. Islam limited the number of wives to four with the caveat that they be treated equitably. The only sexual relations with women outside of traditional marriage permitted by the jurisprudents was regarding female prisoners of war. One should not expect twenty-first century norms to inform jurists of the distant past. In a time when such captives were normally consigned to slavery, Islamic law encouraged marriage or concubinage to provide for their economic and personal needs as an alternative to chattel slavery, for the concubine who bore a child could not be sold. The child was born free, and the mother was freed upon the father's death. Moreover, emancipating slaves was highly encouraged according to the *Qur'an* and Prophetic tradition.

Like most issues, in its jurisprudence, Islam has a well-thought-out practice for polygamous marriages. While only polygyny is sanctioned, the husband is limited to four wives at a time. Islamic law requires that the second, third, or fourth wife inherit equally from the husband. They are to be treated equitably in standard of living, material gifts, and time spent. If the husband is unable to be equitable, the *Qur'an* limits him to a monogamous marriage. Furthermore, it is prohibited for the husband to cohabitate with his wives in the same bed or marry sisters at the same time. Finally, a woman entering into a monogamous marriage has a right to stipulate no further marriages as a condition of the marriage contract.

In a society that exaggerates individualism, polygamy fosters family bonds. The nuclear family unit is fortified with more supportive members to face social ills such as substance abuse, domestic violence, and depression. The extended family model encourages unity, cooperation, and family care in old age (Holder). A polygamous family may potentially fair better under economic hardship, where resources can be pooled, especially when the children are grown and can contribute financially.

Today, the topic of polygamy is mostly dealt with as an issue of religious rights or a lifestyle choice. It is approached by many on a whim. Some consider open polygamous marriages, and even polygamous unions without marriage, as simply a lifestyle choice. In Islamic jurisprudence, there is a rationale for polygamy and how it is practiced. It is to be utilized to strengthen family and social bonds. It needs to be dealt with in a thoughtful manner that can help society to move from one state to a better state.

My interest in polygamy stems from both personal experience and the hypocrisy of Western views on the subject. While I, myself, have not practiced polygamy and have been in a monogamous traditional marriage for over thirty years, I strongly believe it is a necessary and moral practice that should be recognized by US law. As a sermon giver and a counselor of sorts, I promote polygamy as a religious right yet caution against its practice in cases where its implementation causes more harm than good. For example, in a situation where it will cause the breakup of the family through divorce or total alienation of the children, or unbearable societal backlash, I would advise against it. However, it resonates with many people.

A Muslim male client came to my office seeking legal advice on taking on a second wife. I explained that US law prohibits bigamy and does not recognize polygamy. Bigamy is the crime of formally registering a marriage while already married to another person. I told him his bigger problem is how to protect the inheritance rights of the second wife. Since the law doesn't recognize the second marriage under intestate and inheritance laws, the first wife will get everything and the new wife will get nothing. I solved the problem by encouraging my client to add her to his will. In the alternative, I advised him to enter into a contract with the second wife whereby her companionship entitles her to the same monetary benefits she would've inherited under Islamic laws of inheritance. This way, he is respecting the law, which treats the second wife as a girlfriend but, more importantly, fulfills his religious obligation to provide for both of his spouses upon death.

I had a friend who confided in me about marrying a second wife. He openly admitted that taking this step would almost certainly end up in a divorce with his current spouse, and the children would side with their mother. I flatly advised him not to do it unless and until he could guarantee the unity and harmony of his family. Some men are so obsessed by the desire for another woman that they fear committing adultery. In such a situation I would prefer polygamy to adultery.

I believe a society that criminalizes polygamy is by default an adulterous society. I can come up with many reasons why adultery in any of its forms is wrong and detrimental, whereas polygamy can be a solution to certain problems and a source for family unity and harmony. For example, legalized polygamy would guarantee the economic and social rights of all parties, whereas adultery generally entails the betrayal of some parties and leaves others with no legal protection.

Some company owners openly state in their employee handbook that if an employee cheats on their respective spouse, that person will be fired. The rationale is that cheating requires lying and betrayal. If one is not loyal to one's spouse, how could one be trusted or expected to be honest or loyal to the company? Unfortunately, one of the main opportunities for adultery is in the workplace (Imani).

This hypocrisy on polygamy is evident in our immigration laws. The religious practice of polygamy has rendered immigrants inadmissible to the US. Yet, now in America, a US citizen male can petition for his foreign husband to receive the green card. The same is true for a lesbian US citizen. She can bring her wife into the country. However, a polygamist cannot petition the immigration services to bring his second wife. This is a clear double standard and ignores the utility of polygamy as an accepted moral practice.

Therefore, it's an issue of rights. Monogamous and gay marriages allow for spousal benefits in the form of tax provisions, social security benefits, veteran benefits, and others. In addition, the government, especially the federal government, should not be in the business of defining marriage if it allows both monogamous and gay marriages but singles out polygamy. It leads to potential absurdities.

Take, for example, a woman unable to find a husband due to the shortage of men. Legalization of homosexuality while banning polygyny puts her in the position where the only legal means of obtaining the economic and social benefits of marriage are to adopt lesbianism.

The Islamic form of polygamy can offer solutions to problems. Consider the following scenarios. In societies that have recently been involved in war, there are more women than men. The women do not want to be mistresses, engage in illicit sex with married men, or remain celibate. A polygamous marriage is a legitimate option.

A man desperately wants to have his own biological child. His wife of seven years cannot conceive, even after pursuing medical options. The family considers it immoral to hire a woman to act as a baby machine, and even so, they are concerned about parental rights and the fallout of a surrogate mother changing her mind, as well as other potential complications. A second wife to bear their children is a solution.

A wife has a lifetime friend whose husband recently passed away. They are so close to each other that the widow frequents her home and even sometimes spends the night. Over time, she has become a part of the family. However, the husband is off limits to her sexually. To avoid a compromising situation, the three agree to a polygamous marriage.

From an Islamic perspective, polygamy is allowed by all schools of thought. Some consider it as the default ruling. Others consider it as a matter of necessity.

Yet, it is misunderstood, in part, because it is viewed to be in contradiction of women's rights. Some feminists oppose it because it doesn't offer women the same right to multiple husbands. In addition, they say it makes women subordinate to men and they are treated like property.

Women taking on more than one husband has occurred throughout history as well, but it's the exception to the rule. Even with today's liberal attitudes and willingness to push traditional boundaries of what constitutes acceptable lifestyle choices, polyamorous relationships have their own issues of jealousy, child rearing, and long-term problems.

Also, there is a misconception that polygamous marriages are not successful marriages, or that children of such marriages fare worse than children of monogamous marriages. In America, at least, there are not enough statistics to bear this out. However, there is no indication that polygamous marriages would negatively affect the children more than children of gay marriages or single parents. Those who accept gay marriages, in all fairness, must accept polygamous marriages. However, one must keep in mind that the vast majority of Muslims, while allowing for polygamy, practice monogamy worldwide.

Another point to consider is that imposing or enforcing monogamy almost invites infidelity because it is human nature to desire the forbidden. In fact, allowing men to marry more than one woman at the same time demands forbearance and serious contemplation. "Can I afford it? Can I be fair? How will it affect my current family?" Whereas, if you tell men you are confined to one spouse only, you find a tendency toward silent divorces (married on paper, divorced in reality), the breakup of the marriage, or cheating. Catholicism, throughout its history and until relatively recently, prohibited divorce. What did King Henry VIII of England do when his religion prohibited his divorce from Catherine of Aragon? He converted to and started the Church of England, of which he was its head.

Over a thousand years ago, Islam not only allowed for divorce as a last resort but gave that right to women as well. This is not to say that divorce is not an option, but there is a whole world of difference between the divorce of a couple without children and the divorce of a couple with children. If in doubt, ask children of divorces. In Islam, divorce is the most disliked of all permitted things. Thus, if one contemplates avoiding adultery by either divorce or polygamy, even though both are permitted, divorce is worse.

That leaves us with feminist criticisms of Islamic polygamy. Some feminists minimize the fact that entering into a polygamous marriage is by choice, and of economic benefit and security for women who do not want to work outside the home for a living (Lawson). An abusive man will not be any less abusive because he has only one wife. Some feminists view polygamy as oppressing women because they see Islam as generally oppressive to women. However, in Islam, women had the right of inheritance long before their counterparts in the West. Although with more restraints than men, they could initiate a divorce. Upon marriage, a man must give the bride a gift that is hers to keep unless she divorces him without cause. Women kept their maiden names after marriage. Wealth earned, or inherited, is solely theirs to keep. Whereas, the man is obligated to spend his money on the family, including the wife, mother, and female siblings. The major schools of jurisprudence stipulate women are not obligated to be homemakers if they are taking care of the man's rights, and the man can afford domestic help.

Today, many women call themselves feminists. They want the companion of a man but don't necessarily want him around every day. And it makes sense in the modern context where women are given more of an opportunity to reach parity with men economically, educationally, and socially. This may be an appealing arrangement for a woman who is busy and does not want to commit to cohabitating with a husband daily.

These women have received an education, excelled in their careers, and discovered in their late thirties, forties, or fifties that they missed out on family life. They are wealthy and don't need the man's financial support. Therefore, they can dictate more of the parameters of the marriage such as whether to have children or how many, how involved they want the man to be in their lives, and other decisions based on their newly achieved economic and social status. Other women may like the idea of being financially supported by a wealthy man so they don't have to work doggedly to live affluently. For them, a polygamous marriage can be a solution.

It can be argued that Islamic polygamy in America is a bridge between alleviating the constraints of monogamous marriages while maintaining the sensibilities of traditional Christians by rejecting gay marriage. Regardless, is it fair to condemn the Islamic practice of polygamy in a society that allows gay marriages, open marriages, and almost all kinds of sexual activity short of rape and pedophilia?

CHAPTER 3

Zayd

THE ROLE OF ISLAM IN OVERCOMING ADVERSITY
Few things in life bring as much warmth to the heart as seeing a victim of circumstance overcome punishing adversity, an adversity manufactured only in America.

I recently had such a heartwarming experience. It was as if my heart had been cleansed with purifying water, and the residue it left behind was happiness.

Zayd, who got out of prison penniless and helpless five years ago, came into my office with his customary impeccably good-mannered approach, "Peace be upon you."

"And upon you be peace," I said.

Zayd: I hope I am not disturbing you.

Me: Come on in, what do you want?

Zayd: I want to study law and become a lawyer.

Me: You can do anything you set your mind to.

How can I tell you about Zayd?

In America, there is a pronounced tendency to root for and champion the underdog, even under the most unfortunate of circumstances. We don't tolerate having our rights taken away, and we value our freedom. At times, we do take that freedom for granted, and we forget what others have to go through to claim their freedom.

I had seen plenty of situations where practicing Muslims faced extremely difficult situations as immigrants, refugees, or defendants in the American criminal justice system. However, none were as pronounced in my consciousness as the case of "Zayd." The names have been changed to protect the innocent.

In 2010, I received a call informing me of a gentleman in a US jail for some pretty bad charges involving his wife. The caller didn't know what the charges against Zayd were, or maybe he thought I wouldn't take the case if I knew. He pleaded with me to help in any way I could because Zayd had no one in the US. I told him I would do my best.

The following day, I went down to the Alexandria Detention Center, which houses local and federal inmates. I sat down with Zayd to find out his story. He was in his mid-thirties, tan-toned skin with short hair, and clean shaven. He had a heartwarming smile that exhibited his well-kept white teeth.

"As-Salamu Alaikum," I said.

The Islamic greeting of "peace be upon you" stirred something in him and immediately caught his attention.

"Wa alaikum As Salam."

He smiled back with his bright white teeth and gentle demeanor. I told him he must have very important friends because I was called to help him.

He was gripped between the hope of seeing me and the forlornness so evident on his face.

Even for me, a veteran attorney accustomed to hearing tragic and unfair run-ins with the criminal justice system, I was taken aback by his story. I guess mostly because I immediately sensed good in him. He was from Yemen. He lived in Yemen most of his life. He came from a respectable family and formidable tribe. Tribal affiliation is a defining character of Yemeni society. Yemen is known for being one of the poorest countries in the world. It is also a country with a long and well-preserved history. The Romans called it "Arabia Felix," meaning fertile/happy/lucky Arabia. I have known many Yemenis, and I traveled to Yemen for a case in 2013. What I experienced in Yemen confirmed the fond impressions I had of most of the Yemenis I knew.

In general, they are down to earth, happy go lucky, hospitable, and natural entrepreneurs, especially in the South. Zayd was no different. However, he had additional special qualities as well. He came from a very well-raised upbringing. His manners were impeccable, and he was a practicing Muslim.

"Tell me what happened."

He sighed heavily, and this is how he related his story.

"I am from Yemen. I come from a good family. I studied English in Yemen, and like many Yemenis, was enamored by American democracy and culture. A friend of mine told me about 'Hillary,' an American woman who was interested in becoming a Muslim and was looking for a good husband. She was twelve years older than me.

"After meeting her, I was impressed by the fact that she was interested in Islam, would travel all the way to Yemen, and be interested in me. I was hesitant, though. She had two four-year-old twins, a boy and girl, from a previous marriage, and my family was against the marriage. Honestly, she enticed me with her charm and what later turned out to be her lies.

"My wife works for an agency within the Department of State and was stationed in different parts of the world. With her and the children, I traveled to Russia, the Ukraine, and Egypt. Never having left Yemen, or lived in the US, I did not know what to expect of American culture other than what I heard about superficially in Yemen. Her conversion to Islam turned out to be a sham. I don't know if she had been told that Yemeni men are easy going, loyal, and easily manipulated. She was not looking for a husband but more of a paramour and a 'manny' for her children. I thought I would be the twins' father. While she was late at work or off traveling, I took care of the children. I cooked for them, helped them with their homework, played with them, and supervised their activities. More than that, I guided them and loved them as if they were my own children.

"She applied for US citizenship for me. She took care of taxes. She did everything in secret and treated me like a child. She was abusive early on, insisting that everything she did was 'American culture.' She treated me like a domestic servant for her and the children. I treated those children like they were my own. They adored me, but the tension between their mother and me affected them negatively. I tried to instill in them spirituality, modesty, and how to treat others.

"The boy 'Paul' loved me very much, just like the father who was missing from his life. The girl 'Paula' also adored me, but she was heavily influenced by her mother. I was shocked by the promiscuity she was exposed to even before I came into their lives. In the Ukraine, the nanny who took care of them would bring her boyfriend to the house and have sex in the next room where the children could see. Early on, I told the mother that Paula had exhibited sexual behaviors way beyond her years. Hillary would have none of it. She rebuked me for being backward. She said this was American culture. She even said that Paula was just like her, that she could remember as a little girl sneaking out of her bedroom window at night to meet boys without her father knowing.

"I thought that I just had to work harder to make the marriage succeed and show her and my stepchildren through a model practice of Islam that this promiscuity is wrong. I tolerated a lot, but what I could not handle was the mental abuse. Hillary was incredibly ambitious in her career. She was a workaholic and she was obsessed with winning, at all costs. She was controlling over me. I knew nothing except what she wanted me to know. She treated me as if I was stupid and ignorant. My role was to take care of the kids and basically act as the family bodyguard and driver as we traveled and lived in US compounds overseas.

"I can still remember the manifestations of Hillary's attitude and the messaging it must've had on the children. Once, while driving in a US government-provided SUV in the narrow-constricted streets of Cairo, surrounded by smaller vehicles, she shouted at me 'Come on, Zayd! Push through. You know the bigger car wins.'"

I guess this is how American exceptionalism is passed down from one American generation to another, I thought.

"She would not let me complete my studies, which was the single most important priority and dream in my life. Her career came first. And when I applied for a position at the State Department, she laughed at me. She was hostile to the idea of me getting a job because it would interfere with me taking care of the kids even though we had a nanny.

"Our biggest disagreements were over culture, child rearing, and the fact that I was being smothered in her lifestyle. I would threaten to leave and she would have the kids beg me to stay until I relented. I felt trapped. I was depressed and would confine myself to my room on the computer looking for jobs, researching how to apply to schools, and trying to improve my situation.

"In Egypt, it was clear to me that she was having an affair. She would leave saying she was going to work and would not come until the middle of the night or the next day. She had Egyptian male friends who were open with her more than what was normal to me.

"When I was approved for a job with the State Department, she was very angry with me. She almost couldn't believe it. It's as if she felt offended, as if I was escaping her smothering clutches. Things became tense, and I felt vulnerable with her. As I told you, she controlled all aspects of my life and I knew nothing about the American system or its way of life except through her.

"At the same time, we were always fighting over the kids, especially Paula. Once Paula went to school without wearing underpants. I was so upset, and I chided her. What was more distressful was that when her mother found out she yelled at and blamed me. It was the same mantra; this is how it's done in America. She even told me that her sister's family goes around naked in the house and that was normal.

"I was sensing that something bad was going to happen. Her night outings increased, she made threats, and she was more abusive. It was strange. I knew nothing about her private life other than what she wanted me to know. I felt like she was trying to get rid of me. She had me sign documents without understanding what they were for. At one point, she told me I could not drink certain cartons of orange juice because that was for the children, and I would have to drink from what was designated for me. I didn't know what was happening to the point that I once fell unconscious and found myself in another place. Things got scary before they became a nightmare.

"I was later told by a government social worker that I was under domestic abuse."

Being an American and knowing Muslim culture, I could sense the clash of cultures that was taking place. His story built up to this point.

"What brought you here?" I asked, bracing for what was to come.

"One day, after Hillary and I had a fight over her being out late, Paula came to me the next day saying 'Daddy, Daddy, can I see the pictures we took last night?'"

"What pictures?"

"On your digital camera."

"By now Paula was nine years old. I downloaded the photos to my laptop, and I saw pictures of my daughter naked and posing for the camera, along with other pictures of selfies."

When I later saw those photos as part of the evidence, Paula looked jovial while he was in a stupor.

"She was happy and smiling in the photos. There was at least one photo that revealed what appeared to be my hand pulling down her underwear and she was exposing her genital area.

"I was in utter shock. Prior to this, I had told Hillary of Paula's inappropriate behavior. She suggested to me to 'take pictures.' I was so mad at the time. It could be that I took those pictures to prove a point to Hillary. Anyway, I immediately deleted those photos from my laptop. What was strange is that I saw them on my computer again a few months later. Again, I deleted them and after getting a new computer, I thought nothing more of the incident."

"Did you show the photos to your wife?" I asked.

He bowed his head and said sadly, "No."

"That's when my nightmare began. We were stationed in Cairo at the time. While at work I was approached by two FBI agents. They confronted me with the photos. I told them the truth as I told you. I had no idea what was happening to me. I didn't know my rights. I didn't know how to navigate in this system. The agents treated me with utter contempt. They had me sign a confession. I was relieved of my job. I was told to go back to the US. Throughout the whole time, I was in contact with one of the FBI agents. I came to the US with what little money I had and came to Virginia where I did not know a soul, and I was alone. I would call the agent; 'I am here at this hotel. I am running out of money. What's next?'

"I was arrested and charged with production and possession of child pornography."

I knew this was going to be a tough case. Production and/or possession of child pornography is a death knell. The punishment was severe. It involved long prison sentences and lifetime registration as a sexual offender, not to mention the social stigma of such a charge. Zayd was Muslim and the alleged victim was white. Who would believe or understand his circumstances?

So I said, "Look, Zayd. This is a serious crime in America. They will not understand your circumstances. Hillary and her family are white and you are a man of color. The system will not understand, nor is it accommodating. You either take a plea based on the best deal I can negotiate, or you go to trial and let everything come out. Both ways you are facing many years in jail."

He was still obviously confused and in shock. "What I am telling you is the truth."

I had never had to deal with child pornography. As I expected, the system was hell-bent on punishing him to the maximum extent possible.

The prosecutor lied about the evidence the government had and how it was obtained. They let their witnesses lie on the stand. The FBI agent who claimed Zayd didn't call him was setting him up to be lured and arrested in Virginia. When I asked him on cross-examination whether Zayd called him, he repeatedly said, "No."

The veiled racism manifested itself in the sarcasm and laughs Zayd received when he was willing to sit down and explain the story to prosecutors. The truth didn't seem to matter to the lead prosecutor who withheld evidence and was looking to advance her career. Zayd's financial resources were very limited and I ended up getting a fraction of the fee involved in such a case.

The government should be selective when to prosecute, and it should prosecute with honor. What should've been a case of domestic abuse handled internally through governmental services ended up being a witch hunt. He was lured to the Eastern District of Virginia because the government would not have been able to charge him with a crime overseas.

Hillary had taken a nude video of her daughter in the shower. She had told Zayd that her sister and her family customarily walk about the house nude as a family, and that was normal American behavior. It was not clear why she took the video, but it was obvious she was not a normal American. The government was threatening Zayd with more charges because of the "newly" discovered evidence. When the government realized the video was produced by Hillary, the evidence conveniently disappeared. The government was obligated to produce any evidence that could be exculpatory to my client. It is called Brady material. Until this day, I believe in Zayd's innocence and sensed an elaborate coverup. However, I was limited in the resources I could bring to bear in defending Zayd.

Everything happened in Egypt with government officials involved. Those involved chose to handle the situation as a child pornography case rather than a domestic abuse case. In the preliminary hearings, the government put several of its witnesses on the stand, including Hillary. She lied about how she came to know about the photos. I could see the makings of a setup, but, unfortunately, I have to live with the fact that

I could not uncover it enough to save Zayd. Hillary, just days earlier, building up to his arrest, had told him "It will be over soon. Don't worry. I'll take care of things."

When the prosecutor saw he was not willing to accept her version of the events, she pulled every viable deal off the table, leaving Zayd to plead guilty to possession with a potential sentence of up to twenty years. After some back and forth, we agreed to a deal that would potentially give him six and a half years in prison if the judge agreed. Hillary wanted more time for Zayd.

In prison, he was physically abused by one of the guards. One guard pushed him into a wall, other guards placed hand and leg cuffs on him so tightly they caused bleeding and swelling. Others treated him with disdain. When he was willing to sit down with prosecutors to cooperate with them, he was met with laughter and cynicism. Hillary divorced him while he was in jail. She had tricked him into signing a postnuptial agreement. He was not granted bail and was in jail throughout the whole process. It was overwhelming for Zayd.

With the government's continued pressure on him to plead, he eventually decided to plead guilty, thinking it was a release from further pressure. At one point, I filed a motion to withdraw his guilty plea; however, the judge denied it. Zayd collapsed inwardly. As a result of the trauma, he couldn't speak English anymore, and he was not visibly responsive during his sentencing. The judge, with the only mercy he showed, sentenced him to seventy-eight months at a facility with enhanced medical care. The judge, in his sentencing, said, "… the Defendant did not exhibit any proclivity to child pornography."

In spite of this, to Zayd's devastation, later the government would not give him a break on any of his conditions of supervised release.

Zayd spent those seventy-eight months in jail alone and without any help. I received letters from him, but I could not do much for him. However, I was resolved to be there for him when he was released. It was the least I could do under the circumstances. I knew there was more to his case than just the obvious photos. I never thought I would defend a sex offender case. Knowing the system was unforgiving, I resolved to at least give him some hope of redemption. When he was nearing release, I offered my basement as a separate place he could live in, but the probation office refused because I had a ten-year-old daughter living in my home.

I was willing to endure the burden of housing him because he had no other means at that time, and I believed in him. I knew he was not a threat to my daughter. I was looking for a way for him to recover from this tragedy.

After he was released from federal prison, I came to DC to pick him up and took him to the halfway house in Baltimore. He would spend three months there. In the meantime, I was looking for housing for him. To alleviate his situation, I offered him a paralegal position at my office. He was released in December. He would brave the cold winter months to come to my office in Virginia. It would take him over three hours each way Monday through Friday. I was able to find him housing in Northern Virginia. Thus, began his road to recovery.

The law requires sex offenders to register in a national and state registry. His residence and work addresses were made public. He was not yet forty years old. He was estranged from his family in Yemen. He was a US citizen but knew almost nothing about America except through the worldview his wife had exposed him to and through the collision with the American justice system. As a felon, he would not be employable. Because he was on probation, he could not receive Pell grants to finance his dream of higher education.

Zayd never succumbed to hopelessness, even though he flirted with giving up. He prayed quietly five times a day, and openly praised God saying, "My situation could be much worse."

Through a friend of mine, he was able to get a scholarship to study for an MBA. He was elated with this opportunity and made the best of it. Despite the police harassment, he would study long hours in his car, at Starbucks, or at his home. He wanted to make his family proud after the negative circumstances in which he left Yemen. The motivation was especially for his mother who braved an active war zone in Sana to obtain his bachelor's degree and university transcript so he could enroll in graduate school.

She died of cancer while he was studying for his final exams. The government only gave him permission to travel when it was too late, and he didn't have the financial means. Yet he persevered.

During his studies, I encouraged him to get married. Again, he didn't have the motivation, incentive, or finances. However, as part of his religion and Yemeni culture, he was highly encouraged to marry and bear children. Also, he wanted to do it for his mother's sake. Through the local Muslim community, we looked for suitable partners. He wanted to please his family by marrying someone from his country. After a couple of misses, he met a Yemeni girl ten years his junior. Even though they were both in the US, the process unfolded according to Yemeni culture. She came from a very well-respected Yemeni family, clan, and tribe. They asked everything about him in Yemen, from A to Z. They received nothing but glowing reports about his family, his manners, his reputation, and his religious dedication.

From the outset, he explained to his wife and her family about his case, in detail. They appreciated his candidness, and his honesty made him even more attractive to his future wife. They were engaged and married. He finished his MBA within a couple of years, graduating sum cum laude.

When he was released from prison and the halfway house, he was obligated to attend sex offender programs. For him it was torture.

In America, pedophilia and child pornography are a conundrum in Western society. On the one hand, sexuality is exploited and flaunted as evidence of Western freedom and advancement. Yet, pedophilia and child pornography are detested.

The statistics indicate that white males are more prone than other ethnic groups to these deviant sexual behaviors. (West) Some perpetrators were also victims of sexual and other forms of abuse themselves.

Zayd's situation was different and they did not know how to handle it at his counseling sessions. He wasn't sexually abused as a child. The judge acknowledged that he did not have a proclivity for child porn, much less pedophilia. He was socially conservative and was never accused of sexually exploiting the child, even though as the main caregiver he had the opportunity. It was like trying to fit a round piece into a square hole. The government begrudgingly admitted he was traumatized and a victim of domestic abuse with his first wife, Hillary. Even then, no counselor would identify the cultural and religious aspects sufficiently. After a year of individual sessions, he successfully completed the program.

After completing the program, Zayd did the unspeakable in his probation officer's eyes. He had the audacity to have a baby girl with his wife. The baby girl was in the NICU for a week or so. The probation officer did not bother to congratulate the new parents. He didn't even ask about the health of the child. When she got home, he was most concerned that Zayd could not be alone with his new born child. It is understandable that dispassionate professionalism is expected in these situations.

The probation officer struck me as a hapless fellow who was bullied in his life and he was going to bully Zayd, just because he could. Or worse yet, he was put up to it.

It did not matter that the judge found Zayd was not interested in porn, much less child pornography, or that his counselor determined that his offense was situational rather than indicating a proclivity. No, he persisted to terrorize the family in their own home. He threatened to immediately throw Zayd out into the street if his wife did not sign a form he had prepared. It required her to commit to not leaving their child alone with Zayd. Under duress, she signed.

I suggested he file a motion to reduce his supervised release of ten years. As expected, the probation officer would not recommend early termination or remove the restriction of being alone with his own daughter. A friend raised enough money to hire an attorney to work on the motion for early termination of Zayd's supervised release. At this point, Zayd had been under probation for four years with a stellar record. He had no violations during this time, he maintained employment, and married the kind of girl any family would be proud of, earned a master's degree, had a child, and was looking for a little mercy to get back to a halfway decent and "normal" life.

His wife testified that he was a good, loving, and caring husband. As a father, he treated his daughter with the utmost love and gentleness. She told the judge she trusted Zayd, and if she had ever sensed any danger to her daughter, she wouldn't need the government to know how to protect her child. She told him of the burden of having to drive early in the morning every work day to drop off their daughter to the babysitter because they both shared one car.

I was also a witness in support of Zayd. I explained to the new judge (the sentencing judge had retired) how his life was being complicated by the supervised release and the many conditions placed on him. The judge knew that Zayd could not have a computer unless it was fully monitored by the probation officer. He couldn't apply for credit or open a business without the probation officer's permission. He couldn't travel anywhere outside of the geographical location of his area without the officer's permission. I explained to the judge that even his wife's right to stay in the US, known as Temporary Protected Status (TPS), was being held up and her application to become a permanent resident was denied in part because he was still on probation.

I later had to file a lawsuit against the government for the US Immigration Services (USCIS) to approve her TPS.

Zayd had done everything humanly possible to earn early termination of his probation. Even in prison, he took over two dozen educational classes earning twenty-five certificates of achievement. He also left prison with an excellent record. He earned an education, maintained employment, and started a family.

I testified, "Zayd has done everything within his ability to rehabilitate. What more could be expected of him? It's as if the government would be happy if he just gave up and committed suicide."

The judge was visibly perturbed. He interrupted, "... that's not appropriate in this court."

I persisted, "This is my testimony."

He said, "But it's my court and I set the tone."

His lack of hospitality exposed his poor manners. As a minority judge, he might have been intimidated by his peers and felt he had to perform as expected. Or, maybe he harbored some ill will against Zayd. Or, worse yet, he may have been bias and was hiding behind a cloak of justice.

Before the proceedings, we knew the probation officer was going to take a position against early termination. But, why?

The probation officer was always contemptuous of Zayd. He played on his fears, threatened him with additional jail time, and was condescending to him in his interactions with him. For example, once when he appeared for a home visit, Zayd asked him kindly to take off his shoes. He refused. He could have easily put on those shoe coverings that are used in hospitals and by construction workers. In Muslim culture, it is customary to take off one's shoes before entering a home, for obvious reasons; it's hygienic and it's more comfortable and allows for a more natural posture.

It is ironic that one of the precautions suggested by the CDC to minimize the risk of COVID-19 is to take off your shoes upon entering your home to lessen the tracking of germs. Regardless, all that was expected from this government employee whose salary is funded by taxpayers was a little respect.

It is part of the tragedy, though. He gets to know everything about Zayd, yet he is ignorant about Zayd's religion and culture. Zayd gets to know nothing about him and his religion, political views, and biases. Worst of all, we do not know the extent of intrigue against Zayd. Who else is involved? Is his ex still behind his persecution? Is she being shielded by the prosecutors? Is she in touch with this probation officer? Does the judge know about any of this, or is he a part of it?

We do know that he flatly denied his motion. In a long order, he basically said he was lucky to only get seventy-eight months in jail. He further stated that ten years of probation was more than appropriate for his crime. Zayd hadn't sufficiently shown a change of circumstances that would warrant early termination.

The judge also knew that even with early termination, Zayd has to register as a sex offender for many years to come. Thus, the judge was not protecting the public.

Ultimately, his crime was a strict liability crime. This means, by virtue of the event taking place regardless of the circumstances, one is automatically guilty.

In this case, not only is it not clear that he knowingly took the pictures, even if he did, it was under duress from domestic abuse and under highly suspicious circumstances. As the attorney, I had to view the evidence against him. I saw the photos. The selfies with his stepdaughter just were not what one expects in such cases. He looked like he was dazed and confused. If he took the pictures under the influence of domestic abuse, and the probability that he was drugged, that is radically different than a pervert or a person with a proclivity to child porn.

More importantly, what is the use of rehabilitation if one pays his debt to society yet is never allowed to experience the fruits of rehabilitation? He spent years in domestic abuse. He went to jail for over six years and changed his life. He is still under probation, and even if he is released from probation, he still has to register as a sex offender.

This is not a sob story. It is a story of ongoing triumph in the face of adversity. Zayd himself told me, "If I was not a Muslim, I would've either ended up dead or in the gutter left for dead."

His detractors want to see him fail. They want to break his will because he had the audacity to tell the truth and stick to it. Islam does not allow for taking of one's own life as that belongs to God. And, a Muslim believes that any wrong done on Earth will be set right in the hereafter. Yet Muslims are urged to pursue truth and justice. That is why, since his last motion, Zayd has accomplished more equities in his favor; he has purchased his own home.

We will be back, God willing, in front of the judge with another motion for early termination. And, if it's denied, there is always next year and the year after that, and the year after that.

What bothered me about this case was the inability to uncover the almost certain intrigue involved. Without a neutral investigation, we may never know Hillary and the government's hidden role.

Zayd is an underdog, an example of a good person falling into a bad situation. It is the American way to root for the underdog, especially the one who fights on against the odds and succeeds.

That is why I was so happy to see him pursue a law degree.

America should have been for Zayd that uplifting inspiration that Islam clearly was in this case.

CHAPTER 4

Justice Is Not Relative

"Justice in international affairs is absolute because what you know is right for you should be afforded to the other, and when we do things to others just because we can, we know justice has not been served."

—UNKNOWN

Justice can be relative at times, depending on circumstances, but some principles render justice absolute.

For example, say a person steals a dollar from another person, and it ends up in court. The judge rules for the victim but decides the criminal has to pay back ninety-nine cents in restitution. The victim was oppressed by the judge because he was shorted one cent of his right to one full dollar. Justice demands that he receive his entire one dollar. If the victim willingly waives his right to that one penny, that would be his prerogative but not the judge's.

For people of faith, justice is a moral duty one strives to implement. In our current liberal societies, we have diluted the meaning of justice. Not only has it become a relative term and is abused on subjective criteria, it has been twisted to mean the opposite of its definition. One way of understanding the meaning of justice is to define its opposite. "Injustice" is giving something less than it's due.

The penny scenario is a simple illustration of injustice that most of us can accept. But let's consider something less simple.

After 9/11, the government was spying on Muslims looking to justify the war on terror and the human and capital resources allocated to that endeavor. Muslims playing paintball in the woods of Virginia became targets of FBI surveillance. In 2003, eleven young men were charged with various terrorist-related crimes. Some had traveled overseas and fired weapons. No one was killed, injured, or harmed. There was no evidence that America was the target of their paintball training. Most of them received sentences between fifteen years and life.

A couple of years later, a US citizen named Ali Al-Timimi was arrested and charged as the ring leader. He had never been in a training camp, didn't own or carry weapons, and never called for violence against the US. He was an Islamic scholar and a PhD student working on cancer research, and he worked for one of America's Fortune 500 companies. He was charged with various crimes including waging war on America. At trial, he was sentenced to life in prison.

What lessons can we learn from these prosecutions? The people have a right to be free from government oppression, tyranny, persecution, or unfair discrimination. Because this is a democracy, we also have a duty to hold our government accountable and not oppress others in our name. If you are a government official or thinking about becoming one, keep these lessons in mind.

Justice has to be given, even to your enemies.

The great Jurist, Judge Learned Hand said: "If we are to keep our democracy, there must be one commandment: Thou shalt not ration justice."

The failure to show justice even to our enemies becomes our crisis.

If a Muslim had this to say in his allocution at sentencing, it says a lot about our system of justice, and the future of our democracy.

DR. ALI AL-TIMIMI'S STATEMENT AT SENTENCING
13 JULY 2005

All praise is due to God and may God's blessings and peace be upon all his prophets—particularly Noah, Abraham, Moses, Jesus and Muhammad.

Your honor, it is customary at the time of sentencing that those found guilty give a statement during which they admit their guilt and thereupon entreat the court to show them leniency.

I stand before this court having been found guilty of ten felonies. However, I will not admit guilt nor seek the Court's mercy.

I do this not out of any disrespect to the Court. I do this simply because I am innocent.

My claim of innocence is not because of any inherent misunderstanding on my part as to the nature of the crimes for which I was convicted nor is it because my Muslim belief recognizes sharia rather than secular law. It is merely because I am innocent.

Few in the history of this country have been charged with what I was charged. None I believe have ever been so removed from the charges...

During its closing argument the Government read to the jury the preamble to the Constitution. I frankly found it to be a poor recitation. I will not be in any need of paper to recite those words for I faithfully committed them to memory as a schoolboy long before I was taught or learnt any passage of the Koran.

We the People of the United States, in Order to form a more perfect Union, establish Justice, ensure domestic Tranquility, provide for the common defense, promote the general Welfare, and secure the Blessings of Liberty to ourselves and our Posterity, do ordain and establish this Constitution for the United States of America.

I declare the government's recitation poor as it stripped those words of their meaning. Allow me to explain why. The first aim of the Constitution after the immediate raison d'etre—of forming a more perfect Union—is to establish justice. The establishment of justice was mentioned before the aim of providing *for the common defense. Common defense is what we today call security. The reason as to why justice proceeded security should be obvious to all: true security can never be attained without true justice.*

I, as many of my community since 9/11, have been denied justice.

I am not a lawyer so I am unable to cite case law to demonstrate this. I will instead have to appeal to the very philosophy upon which the law is based. Aristotle teaches us that justice means to equate similar things and distinguish between dissimilar things.

Let us recall the crimes to which I was charged: advocating treason, soliciting war against the United States, providing aid and comfort to the enemy, conspiring to levy war against Israel, Russia, India, and Indonesia, and of course at every turn the informal charge of terrorism.

Charges I must say "abounding in crudities and absurdities."

For to accept these charges we must believe that a solitary man who would spend his days working full time at one of Fortune magazine's one hundred best companies and then spend his evenings and weekends engaged in cancer research for a doctorate in computational biology; an individual who never owned or used a gun, never traveled to a military camp, never set foot in a country in which a war was taking place, never raised money for any violent organization would be—could be—the author of so much harm.

"Crudities and absurdities" your honor ... Someone who did not observe the proceedings might justifiably ask: How then was he convicted? The answer, of course, was simply out of fear.

The eminent jurist Stephen L. Carter cautions:

When the secular sovereign decides to try a citizen on a charge that amounts to serving a separate sovereign, the jury should be pressed toward the sobriety of democratic respect rather than the intoxicating fury of the witch-hunt.

If this is his admonition for a charge that "amounts" to serving a separate sovereign, how much more so should it be when the charge is the actual raising of arms against the sovereign!

It is said that historically two trials have captured the imagination of Western civilization. The trial of Jesus Christ and that of Socrates.

Rome was a brutal empire. Athens was a democracy. Plato relates to us that during his trial Socrates said the following:

They—in reference to the prosecutors—are headed by Meletus, that good man and true lover of his country, as he calls himself. Against these, too, I must try to make a defense: Let their affidavit be read: it contains something of this kind: It says that Socrates is a doer of evil, who corrupts the youth; and who does not believe in the gods of the state, but has other new divinities of his own. Such is the charge; and now let us examine the particular counts. He says that I am a doer of evil, and corrupt the youth; but I say, O men of Athens, that Meletus is a doer of evil, in that he pretends to be in earnest *when he is only in jest, and is so eager to bring men to trial from a pretended zeal and interest about matters in which he really never had the smallest interest....*

In the end, I too, like Socrates, am accused and found guilty of nothing more than corrupting the youth and practicing a different religion than that of the majority. Socrates was mercifully given a cup of hemlock, I was handed a life sentence.

Imprisonment of any term, as this Court well knows, is a crisis for the incarcerated and his or her loved ones. I am no exception to that.

But the real crisis brought on by my imprisonment, I sincerely believe, is America's. For if my conviction is to stand, it would mean that two hundred and thirty years of America's tradition of protecting the individual from the tyrannies and whims of the sovereign will have come to an end. And that which is exploited today to persecute a single member of a minority will most assuredly come back to haunt the majority tomorrow.

Thank you.

Ali Al-Timimi, Ph.D Prisoner of Conscience

Fairfax, Virginia July 13, 2005

Some people would say that some criminals, terrorists, or noncitizens do not merit justice. Muslims are held to a higher standard. "O you who believe, stand up as witnesses for God in all fairness, and do not let the hatred of a people deviate you from justice. Be just: This is closest to piety; and beware of God. Surely God is aware of all you do." (Q 5:8)

Fighting for justice may not be an exact science, but it is a mandatory and noble endeavor.

What about justice in politics?

One may think one knows about politics by watching presidential races and observing international affairs. However, you have to play politics to know politics or experience the results of politics. I learned about politics from the case of Dr. Musa Mohammed Abu Marzook.

Dr. Abu Marzook was a Palestinian originally from Yabna, a village overrun by Zionist militias in 1948. He and his family were herded into Gaza. Even then, it was an open-air prison, and while he was able to leave, it only got worse over the next six decades for the people of Gaza.

For the dispossessed Palestinians, obtaining an education is a commandment.

Dr. Abu Marzook studied in Egypt, worked in the UAE, and then came to study engineering in the US in the eighties. While enrolled in a PhD program at Louisiana Tech University, he applied for the Diversity Immigrant Visa Program, also known as the "Green Card Lottery." It has become a controversial program because it allows immigrants from third-world countries who have been historically disfavored from immigrating to the US to become permanent residents by entering a lottery. Since its passage in 1990, over a million and a half immigrants have eventually become US citizens. This program allowed him and his family to become permanent residents of the US.

In 1995, while coming back from an extended absence in the UAE, Dr. Abu Marzook was detained at JFK Airport. After several hours, he was arrested, not for any crime he had committed but at the request of the Israelis. It is called an extradition. Many nations have these extradition treaties that allow participating countries to request their nationals from another country to be handed over to that national's country to stand trial for criminal offenses. Specifically, these treaties exempt offenses that are political in nature.

Dr. Abu Marzook was not being targeted or prosecuted for any crime but for being a Palestinian who was organizing and resisting against Israeli occupation of his homeland. Being one of the relatively few Arab-Muslim attorneys active in the Muslim community, I was identified and tapped by his family and close supporters to work on his case. I had just graduated from law school and moved to Brooklyn, New York. My job was to assist the legal team and help Dr. Abu Marzook in these difficult and trying times.

I wanted the opportunity to work on this case as a law clerk. The first task was to earn the trust of the well-known criminal defense attorney Stanley Cohen. He and Dr. Abu Marzook became very good friends and still are to this day. This friendship of a Palestinian and a Jew puzzles some. It serves to demonstrate that the issues dividing Palestinians and Jews are not race, ethnicity, or religion, rather rights to self-determination and freedom from occupation.

I did my research on extradition and took it to his office hoping to get a clerkship position with him. He was gracious and welcoming but initially wary of my motives. We ended up becoming dear friends and he has been a mentor of mine throughout the decades.

I recall my first visit with Dr. Abu Marzook. He was of medium height, lanky, balding with a beard, and he had a distinct jovial rounded face. He was soft spoken, confident, and very intelligent. Impressed by the heroic resistance of the Palestinians in the occupied territories, I was curious to hear about Hamas from one of its own leaders. Dr. Abu Marzook, at the time of his detention, was the head of the Political Bureau of Hamas. (Justia Law) I learned from him that the so-called "evidence" against him was Israeli propaganda. He was easily able to refute in simple terms the charges against him. In turn, the legal team was empowered to show that his activities were political and not criminal. The Israelis wanted to put pressure on the movement and were using the US and its courts for that purpose.

In the first meeting I had with him, he told me what turned out to be an accurate analysis. The Israelis had no intention of bringing him to Israel as doing so may instigate a Hamas response that the Israelis were not willing to absorb. The whole affair was also a bit embarrassing to the US within the international community because he was being targeted politically (Erlanger).

When the decision of the judge finally came in, we were all sorely disappointed. He ordered Dr. Musa be deported to

Israel to face charges there. We were all hoping for some justice in the case based on its merits.

I was tasked with meeting with Abu Marzook to show him the thirty-page opinion. Despite his political acumen and his revolutionary credentials, he was genuinely upset that he did not receive justice in an American court.

"Peace be upon you," I said as I entered.

His cell was literally a cage. Sometimes, as a form of humiliation or for lack of space, they would put us on the ninth-floor open area that consisted of a ten-foot by ten-foot metal cage that was visible to the officers watching at a close distance.

He said, "And unto you be peace."

He could see the disappointment on my face.

"Judge Duffy has ordered my extradition and dubbed the Palestinian people as terrorists for fighting for their freedom and self-determination."

I was surprised. "How did you know?" I asked.

"I got a call from Stanley. He said you would come to visit with the details."

He knew right away that he didn't want to appeal. "It's not worth appealing. This case is political and it will be resolved politically as it began."

Eventually, his family and legal team convinced him to appeal. However, what he did in the middle of the appeal exhibited his political acumen. He instructed his legal team to withdraw his appeal before a decision could be made by the Second Circuit Court of Appeals.

The unexpected turn of events placed the US and Israel in a precarious position. The Americans expected to extradite him as Israel requested. The Israelis were happy with the long process that kept an enemy of theirs inactive and behind bars, but they weren't ready to have him deported to Israel. How would they try him? The PA and Israel were negotiating turning over areas of control to the Palestinians. Tensions were very high in the occupied territories. Israel had recently been reeling from retaliatory attacks after Baruch Goldstein, an extremist Jewish settler, had gunned down twenty-nine and injured over a hundred other Muslim worshippers in the Ibrahim Mosque in Hebron, known as *al khaleel* in Arabic.

True to Dr. Abu Marzook's prediction, the Israelis declined to accept him.

The Americans, embarrassed by the decision, scrambled to negotiate his deportation to Jordan where he was given a hero's welcome by the then late King Hussein. Being a close ally of the US, and collaborating with Israel, Jordan, which a couple of years earlier had signed a peace treaty with Israel, would be the best place at the time to keep an eye on Abu Marzook and Hamas.

This incident was a crash course in power politics.

The Israelis were willing to embarrass their American allies in court for the chance to play politics with justice. It was a feeble attempt to humiliate Hamas and neutralize one of its leaders for a period of time of twenty-two months. Hamas only became more popular among its people. The Americans, unable to carry out justice, were willing to allow their reputation as a just and free nation to be degraded yet further in the eyes of the people of the Middle East and beyond.

The inability to afford Muslims the benefits of Western ideals of justice goes back before 9/11.

In 1994, while clerking for another well-known attorney, William Kunstler and his partner Ron Kuby, I came into contact with some "infamous" figures: Sheikh Omar Abdel Rahman, Elsayed Nosair, and Mahmoud Abouhalima. Together, they had been charged with a conspiracy case to blow up targets in New York including the Holland Tunnel.

I sat with Sheikh Omar Abdel Rahman in preparation for his trial. The big question on my mind was, what did these men really do? The sheikh said, "Ashraf, assuming everything the government accuses us of doing is true, isn't the Muslim community obligated to ensure we get representation and a fair trial? Assuming we are guilty of the charges, isn't the Muslim community obligated to financially care for our families?"

I looked at him, knowing he could not see me, and said, "Yes, I agree."

Of course, I agreed. He was asking for basic American concepts of justice and due process of law. One does not have to like an accused terrorist, but one should respect the freedom of association enshrined in the Constitution, and fairness dictates we don't punish other than the one who commits a crime.

Growing up, I was a hawk on crime. I believed every criminal should be locked up for a long time.

When I saw the criminal justice system up close, my whole outlook changed. I saw the injustice in the system. The laws were disproportionately targeting minorities, prosecutors were like bounty hunters—convictions were notches on their belts—and judges favored the prosecution at trial and in sentencing. Nothing solidified my convictions over these injustices more than the litany of post 9/11 prosecutions. The War on Terror was a war on Muslims domestically and abroad.

The horrific terrorist attacks of 9/11 pivoted the country and my legal career. As an immigration attorney navigating clients through the complicated web of immigration laws sorely in need of reform, I found myself defending the rights of accused terrorists in high profile cases. Through an intimate exposure to the criminal justice system, and in most cases its utter failure and disparity in policing, prosecution, and sentencing, I identified with John Adams, our second president.

As a lawyer in the colonies dedicated to justice for all, Adams defended the British soldiers accused of massacring American colonists in Boston in 1770. I discovered that if we were going to preserve the rights enshrined in the Constitution, every accused is entitled to legal representation to ensure the system works justly and properly against government abuse.

What made these cases more egregious was the personal connection I had to many of the accused: Shaikh Omar Abdel Rahman, Dr. Sami Alarian, Abdurahman Alamoudi, Ahmed Abu Ali, AbdelHaleem Ashqar, Soliman Elbeheiri, Ismail Randall Royer, Ibrahim Alhamdi, Saeifullah Chapman, Sabri Benkahla, Ali Al Timimi, and many others. In all of these cases, there was either entrapment, unethical handling of evidence, hiding of exculpatory evidence, or political persecution. I had known all of them before their prosecutions, either as friends or acquaintances in the community.

Despite the individual tragedies inflicted on each one of these defendants, their families, and on the Muslim community, Islam's effect shines through in a beautiful way that attests to its power.

Every one of those individuals who were released after long periods of incarceration, as many as fifteen years and more, came back to their communities rehabilitated and mentally intact because of their faith. They were welcomed back into their communities, supported financially and morally. They became gainfully employed, some got married, some obtained educational degrees, and others started new lives outside the US. As far as I know, every single one of them has done well on probation. None of them present a danger to society in the slightest bit. For most, it's just the opposite. They are working, raising families, writing books, involved in activism to help others similarly situated, and overall ideal citizens of our country. Assuming all of these cases were legitimately prosecuted, even the most ardent skeptic would have to admit this is the most ideal outcome. And yet the persecution persists.

Islam challenge's America to live up to its own ideals of justice, for its own sake.

CHAPTER 5

Fasting

Fasting is a personal, empowering, and physically healthy way to lessen greed in our society, and it costs nothing more than an intention and a little willpower. It is a sustained habit of abstaining from food and/or any caloric intake for a given period of time.

The American food industry does not advocate for our health. It is fueled by the desire to accumulate wealth no matter the harm it does to our society.

Case in point: A couple of years ago, Coca-Cola put out a commercial illustrative of its greed, coupled with ulterior motives. The commercial opens with a skyscape of the rising sun emerging from the clouds. Slowly, a caption appears on the screen that reads: "Every year Muslims around the world fast in the Islamic month of Ramadan." It continues, "They abstain from eating and drinking, from sunrise to sunset." It breaks into music and a changed view of a late afternoon skyline on a hot day and a young woman in an Islamic headscarf just missing her bus.

On foot, she is making her way to her destination through a growing crowd of other pedestrians. Along the way she is shoulder bumped by one person and acquires unwelcoming glances from others. Fingering at the headscarf that covers her throat, as if to loosen it from the heat, she continues on her journey. Walking down some steps, she is mocked by a couple sitting on the stairs, with one placing a hoodie over his head in mimicry of her hijab. Tired and distraught, she shakes her head and walks on.

The scene then switches to a white female jogger, bare-shouldered and wearing spandex clothing, her hair pulled back into a tight ponytail, who witnesses the Muslim woman being harassed. She jogs up to a concession stand to buy a Coke. Glancing over to the Muslim woman, she then gestures to the vendor for another bottle and hurries over to the tired girl. Meanwhile, the young Muslim woman walks up to a boardwalk-like rail not far off and looks at the sky. Leaning over, with some relief on her face, she pulls out a napkin filled with a couple of dried dates from her bag.

In silence, the jogger walks over to the Muslim woman and slides one of the open bottles toward her. The Muslim woman looks at the glass bottle and smiles at the Good Samaritan but doesn't drink the Coke. Confused, the jogger raises her bottle to her mouth to drink but then stops, realizing why the Muslim woman doesn't drink, and puts her drink back down. The women smile shyly at each other, and they wait for the sun to set.

The humming fades out and gives way to the lyrics "I'd like to teach the world to sing, in perfect harmony. I'd like to buy the world a Coke, and keep it company." With an exchange of heartfelt smiles, the two women pick up their glass bottles and happily drink their Cokes and share dates, wind rustling through the Muslim woman's hijab and the white jogger's ponytail. Just before the Coke logo pops up on the screen, a final caption reads "What unites us is bigger than what divides us."

At first glance, the commercial appears to disseminate a praiseworthy message: combating prejudice through multiculturalism with positive messaging of unity and education through cultural sensitivity. For the casual consumer, it achieves some of these apparent goals.

However, in reliable studies, sweetened drinks like Coke are linked to tooth decay, type 2 diabetes, and heart disease (UCTV). The beverage industry continues to flood the market with these unhealthy drinks. The higher amount of sugar is added to disguise the taste of the high amount of salt and caffeine in soda. Yes, ultimately, it's a choice. But what does this say about the type of person who knowingly contributes to society's diseases while economically benefiting at the same time? The entrepreneurs who provide healthy alternatives should be credited for their motives and ethics. Coke and other beverage producers can justify their output by pointing to consumer demand. They make money while we get sick. For many, that's an accepted outcome of capitalism.

One of the leading causes of harm and exploitation in our society is greed. Coke is one of many. Take, for example, the food industry, well over a trillion-dollar industry in the US. It's estimated that Americans waste between 30 to 40 percent of the food supply, while others around the globe starve (US Dept. of Agriculture). Small and large businesses alike produce massive amounts of food, and frequently not so edible food products, with one major incentive in mind—increasing their profit margin. This has led to waste, harm to the environment, and a steady increase of disease and sickness in society.

Diseases of lifestyle are enabled and compounded by the readily available source of cheap, chemically preserved, and genetically modified food. Even though the consensus within the scientific community is that GM foods are safe, we do not know what the long-term impact on our health may be. More importantly, in an age where some producers get away with willfully misrepresenting ingredients and amounts on ingredient labels, why would we trust the food sources without reasonable precautions? Fasting is one novel, inexpensive, and measurable effective method of combating all kinds of diseases and health problems stemming from massive food consumption.

Abstaining from food, in differing degrees, is a powerful way to achieve physical health and a sound mind. All the major religions practice a form of fasting. While not an obligation, fasting, for Hindus, is a moral and spiritual undertaking, the objective of which is purification of body and mind and to achieve godly pleasure. In keeping with Buddhist concepts of prohibition and simplicity, a form of intermittent fasting is practiced religiously. According to the Jewish Torah, Moses was sustained on Mount Sinai without food or water for forty days and nights. Jesus is believed to have gone without food for forty days.

Muslims fast during the month of Ramadan. This is a twenty-nine-to-thirty-day dry fast in which one gives up food, water, and sexual relations. It lasts from predawn until the sun sets. Since the Islamic months follow a lunar calendar, Ramadan is ten to eleven days earlier each consecutive year, unlike Western holidays that are usually fixed throughout the year, its complete cycle spans the four seasons after approximately three decades. Imagine celebrating Christmas in June or July! In addition, fasting a couple of times a week is highly recommended.

This healthy practice is not restricted to religious tradition. It certainly began with man's search for food to live, whereby there would be periods of feast and famine in which our first ancestors forayed and hunted for sustenance. Humans are genetically designed and capable to go long periods of time without food. In recent years, intermittent fasting has become popular. Many studies recognize its benefits for sustainable weight loss, immunity strengthening, and longevity (Buchinger). This type of fast can be broken down into several variations and durations. It is generally characterized by a long period of fasting followed by a shorter window of eating, undertaken daily or once to a few times a week.

Long-term and short-term fasting can last from twelve to sixteen hours to forty days and beyond. Longer fasts are scientifically documented to induce what has been identified as autophagy. It's a metabolic process whereby damaged or redundant body tissue is broken down during a fast. The benefits are thought to include the destruction of weak, disease-causing cells like cancer while strengthening healthy cells to increase life span and boost immune health. Fasting is also linked with growth hormone, a peptide hormone that stimulates growth, cell reproduction, and cell regeneration in humans and other animals (Vendelbo).

Its ability to prevent and resolve many health conditions like digestive disorders and certain diseases such as diabetes is no longer disputed. However, the health food industry is unlikely to tell you the road to good health is cemented through the habit of abstaining from food in differing variations and durations.

Apart from discovering its health benefits from religious practice, I stumbled upon water fasting, and it has impacted my life in truly incredible ways. It made me acutely attentive to my body. It led to me incorporating exercise and resistance training as part of a long-term routine. It alleviated and cured certain conditions I had, like acid reflux. It tangibly validated a simple religious practice in my day-to-day life. Fasting in this way profoundly increased my willpower and motivation. And, of course, not to mention extreme weight loss. Fasting for solely weight loss, though, is the least worthy reason to utilize this incredible opportunity, in denying oneself a necessary component of survival to improve one's life.

I began to fast as a religious obligation since I was a teenager. So when I came across water fasting, I already had some experience. I decided to go on a longer fast of a few days to lose weight. I had heard from a friend while on one of my business trips to Saudi Arabia that he went on a thirty-day watermelon fast. He reported losing weight and feeling good after the fast.

In 2006, I began a watermelon fast. It was simple: you can drink and eat as much watermelon as you want. Surprisingly, I ate watermelon and I felt well. After three days of watermelon, I became bored of it and decided to see how long I could go on just water. It lasted another two to three days before I had to stop because I was going on a planned trip to California to visit my immediate family and would not be able to explain, much less justify, not eating.

That began my journey of water fasting. I began to read about it as much as I could. I found some studies on it but not many. Most of my guidance came from the personal stories of what was available on the internet. I separated the wheat from the chaff. I did not fully buy into the detoxification angle. I do believe water fasting cleanses the body, but many practitioners of water fasting take it to extremes without medical research to back it up. Over the years, I progressively worked my way up to longer fasts. My longest water fast lasted sixteen days, and I lost a total of twenty-three pounds.

The bare minimum is for one to experiment with the different forms of fasting and find the most optimum form and duration for your body type, life style, and general well-being. Pay special attention to your gut as gut health is one of the main measurements of overall health according to any ancient medical standards (Ho).

Digestion utilizes a good portion of the body's energy on a daily basis. It requires every single organ of the body, undergoing hundreds of thousands of enzymatic and chemical reactions, to process food and enable energy output. Excessive eating over time takes its toll. Animal studies consistently prove moderate food intake, compared to overeating, leads to longer life spans. Therefore, fasting can be calming, empowering, and regenerative.

Fasting in a fast-paced, stress-laden society that constantly bombards us with readily available "food" can be a powerful vehicle leading to self-control. It also allows one to empathize with those less fortunate. It can help with concentration and boost cognitive function as well.

Unfortunately, not only does the food industry want us to eat and drink as much as our bellies can fit into them, like in the case of the Coke commercial, big companies want to shape the world according to their views. The Coke commercial was deftly produced and deceitfully executed.

Through this commercial, Coke, like other advertisements featuring hijab-wearing women, is appropriating Muslim women's entitlement to articulate their own identities and expressions of who they are and how they want to portray and define themselves, not to fit some Western image of the moderate, benign, assimilated, and Westernized Muslim. There is also a patronizing element to having the physically fit, white, Western-liberated woman extend solace to the distressed, covered, "oppressed," Muslim woman.

The commercial is hypocritical in its political motives as well. On one hand, it champions against bias and prejudice and appears to promote world harmony. Yet, on the other hand, the Coca-Cola company financially supports oppression and violence against Palestinians, operating in and in conjunction with illegal settlements on illegally occupied Palestinian lands in the West Bank. The nonviolent Boycott Divestment and Sanctions (BDS) movement carefully chose ten major corporations to target for their complacency in supporting Israel's illegal occupation. Coke is notably on that list.

Power and wealth, coupled with technology and marketing, are influential tools used for good or ill. One can't expect harmony in the world if one ignores, enables, or commits oppression of others. In another opportunity, Coke even exploited the 2017 Saudi law that allowed Saudi women to drive for the first time by linking this newfound freedom with imbibing Coke. The theme was "Change has a taste to it." Therefore, fasting can become a powerful tool for good, both personally and for humanity.

Fasting benefits include increased willpower, weight loss, clarity of mind, building of self-esteem, much needed empathy, significant financial savings, and more. Not only can fasting tack on healthy years to your life, but it can combat greed.

CHAPTER 6

A Palestine We Can All Applaud

―――

Suppose that a man leaps out of a burning building... and lands on a bystander in the street below. Now, make the burning building be Europe, and the luckless man underneath be the Palestinian Arabs. Is this a historical injustice? Has the man below been made a victim, with infinite cause of complaint and indefinite justification for violent retaliation? My own reply would be a provisional "no," but only on these conditions. The man leaping from the burning building must still make such restitution as he can to the man who broke his fall, and must not pretend that he never even landed on him. And he must base his case on the singularity and uniqueness of the original leap. It can't, in other words, be "leap, leap, leap" for four generations and more. The people underneath cannot be expected to tolerate leaping on this scale and of this duration [...] In Palestine, tread softly, for you tread on their dreams. And do not tell the Palestinians that they were never fallen upon and bruised in the first place. Do not shame yourself with the cheap lie that they were told by their leaders to run away.

Also, stop saying that nobody knew how to cultivate oranges in Jaffa until the Jews showed them how. "Making the desert bloom" [...] makes desert dwellers out of people who were the agricultural superiors of the Crusaders.

—CHRISTOPHER HITCHENS

As a Muslim activist engaged with key players in the Palestinian-Israeli Conflict, about fifteen years ago I was approached by the Swiss government to attend a series of confidential Swiss-sponsored meetings between Palestinians and Israelis. Hamas, the Islamic Resistance Movement, would not directly engage with the Israelis (AFP). Being a Palestinian and having represented Hamas figures, the Swiss were curious to see how "Islamists" would engage in peace-building measures. Since I was a Muslim but not a Hamas member, I was invited to participate.

Here I was in Switzerland, face-to-face with a former head of the Mossad. His reputation preceded him. He had overseen high profile assassinations (and attempts) of Palestinian leaders. Characteristically expressive as I am, I didn't sense the discussion heat up in time. In mid-speech—as I was articulating why, at the end of the day, the Israelis would have to undergo painful compromises for peace, some twenty years my senior—the former spy chief bursts out "Shut up! Shut up!"

My words landed on a sore spot for him. I froze, but not out of fear because we were in a safe space. However, instinctively, I bolted to my feet, kicking my chair back in fight-or-flight mode. For a moment, the room of about seventeen people went silent. Immediately, the Swiss Ambassador moved toward me as if to get in between me and the former Mossad chief, who was halfway across the room and with tables in between. Others followed suit to calm the situation down. However, there was no real threat of a physical altercation. As I sat back in my chair, out loud, I questioned, "Is this how the Israelis act?"

Thus, I was thrown headlong into the fray of politics, and what has been branded as the intractable Palestinian-Israeli conflict.

My Palestinian colleagues were bewildered and fearful for me, for it seemed I stood up to one of the most intimidating personalities in the Palestinian-Israeli conflict. Later, I learned that his bodyguards, who insisted on being present in the Swiss brokered meeting room, had impulsively placed their hands on their concealed sidearms during the confrontation. I have to admit, in the heat of the moment, I was a bit amused that these awe-inspiring figures of Zionism, and the establishers of the modern state of Israel, with their American super power-support, nuclear weapons and advanced technology were rattled by me, a nonviolent Palestinian-American from Chicago making a passionate argument for Palestinian self-determination.

However, the truth was I reacted out of weakness, not being familiar enough with politics. I was raised to be respectful to my elders. Vulgarity was antithetical to my religious training. Yet, seasoned politicians do not always share the same ethical standards. The "appropriate" political response would have been to respond in kind—"No! You shut up!" That's the tone most politicians understand.

However, by detaching politics from religion in this way, we unwittingly create schizophrenic behavior, one that leads to exploitation, corruption, and unjust results. The religious are expected to be meek, accommodating, and ethical while the politicians are allowed to be Machiavellian, amoral, and aggressive.

Islam, more than a religion, is a way of life. Therefore, the adherent isn't expected to compartmentalize his or her life between the sacred and the profane. That is one point the Swiss picked up on about the Muslim participants. While we didn't drink alcohol, we didn't prevent others from consuming it. We had no problem weaving in and out between our justifications for our positions based on international law and theology. One theme cut across both lines and that was justice. Where is America in living up to justice when it comes to the issue of Palestine?

The conflict is a very sensitive topic here in America as well because the parties involved have so much invested in the status quo, and the ultimate outcome (Sharp). However, it is incumbent upon those who value justice and freedom to speak out and take the necessary actions to bring about a just resolution to the conflict.

The parties in America directly affecting the situation in Palestine and Israel are the Jewish-American community, elected representatives on the local and national level, institutions of government, and mid-level government career employees like those in the state department, right-wing Christian and evangelical groups who have aligned their support for the Israeli state to match their eschatology, the return of Christ, and end times (Martin). Organically, there is a growing public and active support for the rights of Palestinian self-determination coming from other religious groups including Muslims, Christians, Jews, students, and the young (Telhami). This backing is reflected in a new cadre of elected officials who openly oppose Israeli apartheid and voice support for Palestinian rights (Bennis). It wasn't always that way.

The stakes are high. The US has invested greatly in this conflict economically, politically, and psychologically (Washington Report). The Jewish-American community may be divided on many things, but historically, through hard work and organizing, it has been united in engineering complete and unwavering US support for Israel. As the Jewish-American community ages, its younger generations become less attached to the call of the Zionist experience. It is difficult to be young, Jewish, progressive, and believe in pluralism, and accept or justify the plight of the Palestinians. There is a palatable expanding rift in Jewish positions on the Palestinian-Israeli Conflict. While there is a growing cadre of Jewish supporters for Palestinian rights and self-determination, it is unfortunate that a segment of the Jewish community, and through their organizations, are a main generator of the Islamophobia industry (Bazian).

Pro-Israel lobby groups and their supporters view pro-Palestinian activists and their activism as a threat to their interests in supporting, defending, and funding Israel. The policies of Israel and its occupation has caused a rift between right-wing Jewish groups and otherwise allied groups like Muslims and moderately progressive groups.

The US is a majority Christian nation (Pew Research). Of the Christian population, the majority is of a protestant denomination. The Christian Right boasts millions of followers, and they have made their voices heard throughout government (Brenneman). Broadly, they are referred to as Evangelical or Born Again. In addition to their conservative views on such issues as abortion, gay marriages, and prayer in school, they are staunch supporters of the state of Israel. Many of these Christians believe that support for the state of Israel is a prerequisite to the second coming of Christ. They believe it's a fulfilment of prophecy (Bump).

Yet, these same Christians view Jews in a negative light. They still bear the old prejudices of Christian Europe that the Jews rejected Christ. It is odd that the Jewish state Christians support is hostile to religion in many ways. Unlike the rule of King David, modern Israel is a secular state. Homosexuality, pornography, usury, and atheism are an integral part of the social fabric that makes up the current state of Israel (Auerbach) (Arlosoroff) (Tourist Israel) (Haaretz). One does not have to believe in God to be Jewish (Rosove). Yet, some make a religious claim to Jewish rights to Palestine. It is also telling that while these same Christians profess the peaceful message of Jesus, they support Israel's brutal repression of the Palestinians, including the Christians of the Holy Land. They are, as a group, staunch supporters of America's wars and intervention in the Middle East (Cook).

This, in part, explains the paradox of Western Christianity (Bethancourt). Jesus as a messiah was expected to appear as a warrior king to overthrow Roman rule, liberate the Jewish people, and sit on the throne of David. Because this did not happen in his lifetime, he was rejected by most Jews, but it forced early factions to adopt a new theology, and a meek and timid approach to the overbearing Roman state. "Give to Caesar the things that are Caesar's, and to God the things that are God's." (Mark 12:17)

Christ's imminent kingdom would now have to be deferred to a distant future. It lasted only until the conversion of Constantine to Christianity, in the fourth century CE (DailyHistory). Now, the faith had a sword in which to indirectly wield its power for Christ (Heather). Yes, a sword, as the word is replete (mentioned over four hundred times) in the *Bible*. Colonial projects since the Crusades were characterized by a distinctive pattern (Stanley). Israel was the last in a series of Western colonial projects.

The secular state would conquer and colonize, and the Church would accompany mostly in harmony with the state to convert the native populations (Comaroff). No doubt the church and state used each other for their own purposes (ICT Staff). While the native population was being exploited, robbed of its natural resources, and murdered, the men of the cloth were preaching the kindness, love, and peacefulness of Jesus (Andrews). This is the nature of politics in the West. The colonizers were basically slapping with one hand while shaking with the other. It was an effective formula for the colonizers, yet flawed for the native populations.

America was no exception, albeit farther removed from the colonial past of Western Europe, conversions in Korea, Vietnam, and Latin America follow a similar pattern. Converting to Christianity was an economic benefit. A strengthened post-World War II nation, America was seen as a savior, and Christianity as a source of strength and wealth (Hazzan).

By merging the sacred and the profane, Muhammad was incredibly effective in laying the foundations for Muslim governance early on. What was considered "politics" now had to be tempered by religious and ethical standards of behavior. Based on Islamic religious sources, Muslim jurists had to develop a complex body of law governing war, slavery, and rule over Muslims and non-Muslims. Muslim civilization was able to bring together temporal and spiritual rule in a unique way.

In Christianity, such an advanced body of precedent did not develop in the same manner because, supposedly, Christianity was not founded by a "warlord" like Muhammad. Christian jurisprudence developed under Catholicism when the Church served as both the religious and temporal power of the state. However, even then, in Christianity, Jesus came to alleviate the mosaic law. For Christians, unlike Muslims, the law was more facilitative, not constitutive (Movsesian). However, the Crusades were a result of a deeply Christian Europe. And for some controlling the Holy Land has long been a Christian aim.

The American experience was supposed to be different. Like the early followers of the Prophet Muhammad, they had fought a war of liberation. However, Christianity informed the views of our forefathers. It did not rule the United States. The division of church and state was reflected in the First Amendment to the Constitution. Referred to as the Establishment Clause: "Congress shall make no law respecting an establishment of religion, or prohibiting the free exercise thereof; ..." (National Archives) America was founded by Christians for Christians. It worked when America was more homogenous. Despite the mandate to separate church from state, in reality, it was not actually effectively accomplished.

Thus, one of the challenges for America is to live up to the promise of freedom and justice for all. No better opportunity presents itself than a just stand when it comes to the Israeli-Palestinian conflict. The Palestinian cause is deserving of the American nomenclature of allying itself with the underdog. However, when it comes to Palestine, the spirit of justice is lacking.

Why were elected officials, many progressive Jews, and "prosperity gospel" Christians turning a blind eye to the well-documented oppression of the Palestinians (Bruton)? Well over a decade into the 1993 Oslo Accords, it became clear that the negotiations were not only a failure but further entrenching Israel's occupation. Negotiators talked, but Israel's settlements expanded. The dispossession of Palestinians from their homes and lands continued (University of California Press).

It's been over a decade since I attended the Swiss-sponsored meetings to foster peace. Now I witness grassroots efforts of Americans coming together and standing for justice. The landscape is rapidly changing.

From trial balloons like President Carter's book, *Palestine: Peace Not Apartheid*, to Representative Ilhan Omar questioning blind congressional support of Israel's illegal occupation,

American public opinion has been incrementally shifting toward a recognition of Palestinian rights (Carter).

A growing number of evangelicals have shown a willingness to be educated on the Palestinian narrative. Jewish-Americans with a comprehensive sense of *tikkun olam* organize in support of Palestinians and make the sound argument that criticism of Israel and its policies do not equate to anti-Semitism (Lerner). Even lawmakers are now willing to openly support Boycott Divestment and Sanctions (BDS) despite the lopsided influence of the Israel lobby (Pink).

Living in America and experiencing individual freedoms, as constricted as they have become, has empowered many Muslim immigrants to overcome the victimization mindset of colonialism. That is one of the reasons I was able to sit down face-to-face with the very people who were responsible for the Nakba. The Nakba is what contextualizes the Palestinian struggle for freedom. It is also the starting point that most Israelis and many Jewish Americans and their supporters ignore when it comes to a sincere and genuine effort to solve the conflict at its roots.

Neither the US nor Israel can tolerate using 1948 as a reference point.

In that fateful May of 1948, some 750,000 millennia-old dwellers of the Holy Land, both Muslim and Christian, were expelled from their homes, never to return. Many of those hapless families, men, women, children, and the elderly, marched for days to escape the death and destruction of the invading Zionist militias. This catastrophic loss of their homeland is what the Palestinians call the Nakba (Pappe).

My actions would have been unbeknown to the Swiss. I had managed to get major US newspapers to publish op-ed pieces for Hamas leaders (al-Zaha). At the time, and arguably today, it would have been considered material support of terrorism except that the statute of limitations has run out (Cole). Even though the engagement in freedom of speech was to bring about peace. One of the op-eds I coordinated coincided with President Carter's trip to meet with Hamas leaders. My contact at the Carter Center asked me about the op-ed as *The Washington Post* ambushed President Carter in its own editorial that day.

It began "ON THE OPPOSITE page today we publish an article by the 'foreign minister' of Hamas, Mahmoud al-Zahar, that drips with hatred for Israel, and with praise for former president Jimmy Carter (Washington Post Editorial)."

I was so disappointed in the state of affairs in this great country when I heard Prof. David Cole's oral arguments before the Supreme Court in *Holder v. Humanitarian Law Project*, a Supreme Court case deciding the extent to which freedom of speech could be criminally prosecuted as providing material support to terrorism. Only God and I knew that the exchange between Prof. Cole and the late Supreme Court Justice Anthony Scalia was in reference to the secretive work I had done.

David D. Cole

—So, for example, under that view, The New York Times, The Washington Post, *and* The LA Times, *all of which published op-eds by Hamas spokespersons—Hamas is on the list—thereby providing a benefit to Hamas, working with the Hamas spokesperson, they're all criminals.*

President Carter—

Antonin Scalia

Well, we—we can cross that bridge when we come to it.

David D. Cole

—But—

Antonin Scalia

This is an as-applied challenge, and we are talking about the kind of advice and assistance that your clients want to give.

David D. Cole

—Right, and, Your Honor, there's no—

Antonin Scalia

It's not a New York Times editorial.

David D. Cole

—Well, it is, though.

It is, Your Honor.

I mean, it's—Ralph Fertig is not The New York Times, and he's not President Carter, but it's the same sort of support, right?

President Carter—

Anthony M. Kennedy

No, no.

I thought that he was—he wants to meet with the people.

The New York Times didn't meet with Hamas to tell them how great their editorial was.

David D. Cole

—No, but it's not about—it's not about whether you meet with them.

It's about whether you coordinate with them, and they've certainly coordinated with the Hamas spokesperson in editing and accepting and then publishing his editorial.

That is—that would be providing a service.

It would—

Antonin Scalia

It depends on what "coordinating" means, doesn't it?

And we can determine that in the next case.

David D. Cole

—Well, let me—let me also answer it this way, Justice Scalia: If you look at the specific speech which our clients seek to engage in, it includes writing and distributing literature in conjunction with the Kurdistan Workers Party in the United States advocating their support.

How is that different from The New York Times?

While it was my idea and execution, it was by God's grace and the help of others that I pulled it off. Unbeknownst to me while I was assisting one of my clients to place an op-ed in *The Washington Post,* he was working with another person to place a different article on the same topic with *The New York Times.* Both submissions got published on the same day. The Israel first crowd were up in arms, and the news wires called it a media coup (Debusmann). It may never have happened that the same op-ed contributor published a submission on the same day with the two most well-known newspapers in America.

Hamas is considered a terrorist organization by the US, Israel, Europe, and those nations aligned politically with them. However, Hamas is an Islamic movement that won legislative elections that the Bush administration insisted on holding. They just didn't like the results (Judis). However, Hamas is a legitimate voice of the Palestinian people. They sought to engage with their enemies for the sake of avoiding bloodshed, overwhelmingly Palestinian blood.

Hamas' engagement with Western media, and indirectly with the Israelis, elucidates a well-conceived Islamic precept. Negotiating with your enemies is not prohibited, rather negotiating in bad faith is forbidden. In the context of the Palestinian issue, it means that Mahmoud Abass, Palestinian Authority (PA) President, who is beholden to Israeli and American interests is not qualified or eligible to negotiate on behalf of the Palestinians. He cannot be said to be working in the best interests of the Palestinians. It is a matter of trust. One must have trust in one's leader for such a leader to enter into negotiations with one's enemies that will bind the parties and their respective constituencies. Islamic jurisprudence would not prohibit negotiating with one's enemies as long as principles were maintained (Scham).

Since I was a private person, I had no problem in meeting with Israelis, specifically since none of the participants were directly speaking on behalf of the Olmert Government at the time. I was also representing myself and not the Palestinian people.

In participating in these trust-building sessions and reverse role-playing workshops, I recognized that culturally we had a lot in common. I heard the narratives of former and current Knesset members representing the spectrum of political parties, retired generals, religious figures, past Israeli negotiators, and representatives of the settler movement. Their personal stories of Zion crystallized my just struggle for Palestine.

In one of the reverse role-playing sessions, I was given the role of a young Jewish settler. As a Jewish settler, in a few minutes, I was supposed to justify settlements. It was an extremely easy task (not justifying the settlements but playing the role). Like most Americans, I have been inundated with the Zionist propaganda in the media and halls of power.

I basically said "we" the Jewish people have a five-thousand-year-old calendar. We are intimately tied to the land of Israel given to us by God to Abraham and his descendants through Isaac and Jacob (later to be named Israel). The Arabs have some twenty-two Arab countries and we poor Jews have only one. Judea and Samaria are our land, so we are just populating our land. The Middle East is a region of danger and barbarity, and we need a safe enclave to live free from persecution. After the Nazi Holocaust, we were able to establish the only democratic state in the Middle East. Oh, and as for the Palestinians, they can cross the border and live in Jordan where most of the population is Palestinian.

Ironically, the Israeli participants had a much harder time articulating the Palestinian narrative. After the break, I came upon a group of the participants talking. A former general stopped me and said, "Ashraf, I was just telling my colleague Akiva here that you did a better job articulating the settler position than the settlers themselves." She was one of the more liberal participants, and we all chuckled.

However, it became clear to me that the anti-Semitism of Europe could not be solved by committing another wrong—that of dispossessing the Palestinians of their homeland.

I am not going to call it ethnic cleansing, even though it's widely accepted as such. The 1948 displacement of Palestinians from their homes was illegal, immoral, and a crime. The

Palestinians have a right to return and have a right to resist militarily. The 1967 Israeli occupation of the West Bank, Gaza, and the Golan Heights of Syria is illegal under international law. Therefore, the settlements are illegal and an obstacle to peace.

Therefore, honoring the Nakba is honoring justice. I believe America should be aligned with this noble struggle for freedom. The Nakba is the struggle for a nation state, the need to live in dignity, the right to be free of occupation, and live peacefully. It commemorates hope and the fight for freedom and justice, which is the American way.

I know it is difficult for my Jewish cousins to read this and challenging for many Americans to comprehend. However, I do not see the continued existence of the state of Israel beyond the next generation of twenty years or so. I have five main reasons for this confidence.

1. American focus is diminishing. American support for Israel runs deep and to the tune of over $230 billion over the past seventy years (Sharp). You will continue to hear staunch rhetoric from politicians in support of Israel. However, the actual support will fall short of the oratory. As America becomes more divided and attentions turn inward to domestic matters, US support for Israel will wane. The young, progressive, Jewish community will lead the charge for Israeli accountability. Older Jewish-Americans will become less and less influential over time.

This will provide for a creation of new facts on the ground that will not be favorable to Israel.

2. The simple demographics will place Israel in an untenable situation. The Palestinian population of Israel proper, the West Bank, and Gaza is nearly seven million (Cortellessa). The current Jewish population is 6.8 million (Jewish Virtual Library). Israel will rule over an apartheid state of which Jews will ultimately be a minority. It is expected that the Palestinian population will continue to overtake the Jewish population. While some Israeli shills float kicking Palestinians out of the West Bank, such a drastic measure would actually hasten the demise of Israel. In the long-term, ruling over a hostile majority will not be sustainable.

3. Existential threat of water scarcity (Obidallah). Right now, Israel siphons water from underground aquifers on Palestinian nominally controlled territory in the West Bank. This water is used to supply the very settlements that have encroached on Palestinian land over the past fifty years. While settlers have water to stock their swimming pools, the Palestinians are relegated to drinking polluted water. The situation in the near future is only expected to get worse (Amnesty). Whereas Israeli settlers can move to Israel proper or emigrate to the US, for example, the Palestinians have nowhere to go.

4. The "Arab Spring" and self-determination. Even though the Arab uprisings of nearly a decade ago have been quashed by Arab regimes, with US, Western, and Israeli backing and support, the dismal political, social, and

economic factors that fomented the "Arab Spring" are still present and getting worse. America could not win in Iraq or Afghanistan. Similarly, Israel as a super power could not destroy Hamas in Gaza, and will not be able to militarily crush every single threat forming on its borders in Egypt, Jordan, Syria, and Lebanon when the second round of Arab revolutions come. They will come because the Arab world has been consistently prevented from electing Islamic movements (Ahmad). Therefore, the possibility of Islamic governments coming into power will become greater in the future. A change of governments in Egypt or Jordan, which both have peace treaties with Israel now, can be a game changer. Egypt, for example, with Israel, maintains a brutal blockade of Gaza. It was alleviated by President Morsi, the first and only freely elected president in Egypt's history.

5. Israel's own right-wing policies are jeopardizing the existence of the Jewish state. Netanyahu and the Israeli right are pushing the boundaries of the good will Israel has earned over the years with the Jewish diaspora, lobbying efforts in America, and Christian communities. As the world insists that the settlements are an obstacle to peace and must stop, the Israeli right continues to acquire more and more illegally occupied territory for its settlements, creating realities on the ground that will preclude a future Palestinian state, and therefore, a lasting peace to the Palestinian Israeli conflict.

Like responsibly dismantling America's empire, the youth of our country must play a positive and key role in bringing about a fair, real, and lasting peace between Israel and the

Palestinians. It is the American way. If the older generations can't get themselves to confront the roots of the conflict, the younger generations can do a better job. The monumental injustice of 1948 has become seventy-three years old. Let's not wait until 2048 to rectify the slow motion "ethnic cleansing" of the Palestinians.

I leave you with this poem dedicated to Jerusalem and the Holy Land.

O' Jerusalem

Jerusalem, with a towering church steeple,
O' Ye beautiful city of many people.

Where the proud domed Aqsa Mosque stands tall,
Where Jews worship at the Wailing Wall.

Yet this city so proud and old,
By so many hands controlled.

From Canaanites to Philistines, Diverse peoples and changing scenes.

Across its fertile and forsaken landscape, pharaohs fought Hittites,
And Phoenicians, Assyrians and Persians traversed its holy sites.

The Children of Israel had their hour,
Under King Solomon wealth, like rivers, flowed.
But the Babylonians assumed power,
For God's "Chosen People" reaped what they had sowed.

The city was conquered by Alexander the Great,
Until the Romans handed it yet another fate.

The proud and noble Arabs protected it against invaders,
letting the Jews return.
Until the wrath of the Christians brought the Crusaders,
who displaced them without concern.

Saladin, the Kurd, in noble fashion again liberated the city,
the Jews were welcomed back.
Simply to be inherited by the Mamluk slaves of antiquity,
still they remained free from attack.

For four hundred years the Ottoman Turks allowed Jerusalem to mend and expanded its walls.
Upon occupying it, the British General Allenby declared
"today to the Crusades it falls."

The Empire of the set-less sun administered it
with impunity,
Mandated a land for one people to another without authority.

Europe's longsuffering Jews colonized the land,
Uprooting its inhabitants from the sand.

Palestine "A land without people for a people without land,"
they said.
Tell the millions made refugees, those at Deir Yassin, and
the thousands dead.

Palestinian blood is a witness to the Holy Land's gene pool.
Who would deny them of their indigenous birthrights save
a fool.

I am proud to say that Jerusalem is the city of my birth,
But as long as my people cannot live in Palestine what is
it worth?

It's worth everything dear, yet it's not the land we revere.
It would be nothing without the cause to which we adhere.

The world marvels at rockets fired from Gaza not realizing,
A fifth generation refugee aims at what was once his home.
Akin to the Heroes of the Warsaw Ghetto uprising,
They remind us freedom is more powerful than any
"Iron Dome."

In peace, Jews are welcome from the Euphrates to the Nile,
Or rule over an apartheid state or live in exile.

Long before Ancient Rome's occupation the Arabs roamed
the Holy Land.
Long after Israel's occupation, like deep rooted olive trees
they shall stand.

Jews reject Christ, they and Christians deny our
beloved Prophet.
But to him, Moses and Jesus are his brothers as God saw fit.

Since Adam built the second house Al-Quds has been a
Muslim trust.
As long as God wills, it will be in the hands of those who
are just.

Practice here at home what is preached abroad.
America raise your hand to be seen,
And stand up in justice for Filisteen,
A free Palestine we can all applaud.

CHAPTER 7

Islam and Christianity

"...the religiosity of Muslims deserves respect. It is impossible not to admire, for example, their fidelity to prayer. The image of believers in Allah (God) who, without caring about time or place, fall to their knees and immerse themselves in prayer remains a model for all those who invoke the true God, in particular for those Christians who, having deserted their magnificent cathedrals, pray only a little or not at all."
—POPE JOHN PAUL II, VATICAN CITY, *RELATION OF THE CHURCH WITH NON-CHRISTIAN RELIGIONS*

We are at a crossroads in Christian-Muslim relations. If it was up to me, I would like to engage in a loving and respectful relationship with Christians. By default, Islam encompasses many of the teachings and beliefs embedded in Christianity and Judaism. Muslims believe in one God who created Adam and Eve, sent many messengers and prophets to call people to the one true God, and bestowed upon Jesus special status, e.g., born of the Virgin Mary, was sinless, is the Messiah, is one of God's greatest prophets, and will return to usher in a period of justice and righteousness.

Islam also recognizes the authenticity of previous revelation. We believe Moses and Jesus were given scriptures. I would like to be able to benefit from the Torah, the Gospel, and Qur'an. Although I believe in Jesus and Moses, Jews and Christians do not believe in the Prophethood of Muhammad.

On that basis many people choose Islam.

One of the most frustrating things I face in my humble contributions in helping to reform American society for the better is dealing with right-wing Christian individuals and groups. As people of faith, we have so much in common, and at least for the socially and politically conservative, we share a similar stand on many issues.

I strongly believe that if you, as a young person or an individual in a position of power, truly care about the future of our country, you would uphold these three equally important positions:

1. Nonintervention in the affairs of other countries. This is not isolationism. We should maintain good relations and trade with the rest of the world, but we should responsibly dismantle the empire before the blowback of our policies lead to a violent crumbling of our power.

2. Upholding the Constitution and safeguarding our liberties. My fellow Americans enjoyed a false sense of security when they witnessed me being singled out for additional security at airports after 9/11. Albeit, in a different context, Benjamin Franklin said "Those who would give up essential Liberty, to purchase a little temporary safety,

deserve neither Liberty nor safety (Siegel)." The Snowden revelations and everything we know about our government shows us we are all being spied on, and, slowly, our liberties are being compromised. Muslims are the canary in the coal mine. What is affecting Muslims since 9/11 in the loss of liberty will affect all Americans unless we do something about it.

3. Treating the national debt as a moral issue. We can't continue to just print money as a way to solve our economic problems. Our generation may get away with it, but what about our children and their grandchildren? We owe it to them to be fiscally responsible. I for one do not want to be damned by my children or grandchildren when they are handed a financial disaster. Coming generations will wonder what we did with all this money when we had it, and they will learn that we spent trillions on Iraq, Afghanistan, and the War on Terror (CNBC).

Five members of my family and I went to the primary polls in 2012 and voted for Ron Paul. He was huge on these three issues. He wanted to defund Israel and other nations from American foreign aid. He consistently voted against the Patriot Act, which has been an affront to our civil liberties. And he wanted to abolish the Federal Reserve and introduce fiscal responsibility.

However, when I repeatedly called and emailed his institute to establish relations with conservative Christians, I was completely ignored. Some Christians will have nothing to do with Muslims even though we may share a lot in common and agree on many policies to reform America.

When it comes to religious beliefs, I contend there is only one truth. It is obligatory upon each person, according to one's ability, to search for that truth. Even if a person spends one's entire life looking for that truth, God will judge such a person according to one's intentions and how one acts upon those intentions. Sincerity of intention is paramount. It transcends rigid ideology or belief. Sincere and just-minded individuals, regardless of race, religion, nationality, or ethnicity, are more akin to each other than disingenuous and unjust individuals, irrespective of their tribal affiliations.

Muslims totally reject trinity and the divinity of Jesus. Christians totally reject the prophethood of Muhammad. However, sincere Muslims and Christians find it easy to relate to one another. For Muslims, Christians are "people of the book" and closest in friendship to Muslims because many of them are spiritually humble. For sincere Christians, loving Muslims is a tenet of their faith. The insincere and arrogant, and more often than not ignorant, among Christians in America despise and denigrate Muslims. I come across them on a regular basis.

Although considered a social taboo in the professional setting, I do not shy away from discussing politics and religion whenever the opportunity avails itself. I like to engage persons of all walks of life on these topics to discern what their views are and why. Once, riding in an Uber, I engaged a reluctant white male evangelical Christian in discussion. I told him he and I had a lot in common. We both believed in God, accepted the same prophets, and sought to do good works. I said the major difference is I did not believe in the divinity of Jesus.

He was irritated and asked, "Are you a Moslem?"

I said, "Yes, I am a Muslim."

"Then we don't believe in the same God," he said. "Your god is a pagan god, and your prophet is a pedophile."

I was amused because I assumed he was getting such polemics from either Islamophobic propaganda or his pastor. Had I not engaged him in conversation, I would never have known his true feelings, or where they were coming from. He went on to profess how much he loved me. With love like that, who needs enemies? In his ignorance and arrogance, he may have thought I would be attracted to his faith.

The objective of Christian Islamophobes who carefully craft a narrative that Islam is a barbaric faith that encourages terrorism, violence, sexual assault, abuse of women, and pedophilia is to incite fear and hatred of Muslims. These Christian leaders view Islam as the threat from within. Muslims worship the same God, recognize the same prophets, and profess to have the truth. Therefore, it is strategically necessary to undermine Islam's credibility with the masses of Christians by claiming Muslims do not worship the same God of the Old Testament and vilify the Prophet Muhammad to detract from his message. The remedy to this fear-mongering is for Christians to get to know Muslims personally, and for Muslims to go out of their way to engage with Christians and others.

It wouldn't be fair to lump all Christians in one basket. Irrespective of the denomination of Christianity, the determinative factor of how any given Christian acts is determined by one's sincerity and sense of fairness. In that vein, it was refreshing to see a white evangelical Christian express love and friendship for Muslims. Pastor Bob Roberts breaks the mold. In discussing Christian-Muslim relations, I sensed an environment of sincerity in the pastor's overtures. He is the pastor of an evangelical church in Texas.

He publicly put out a video entitled "Why Evangelicals Hate Muslims."

He gave three convincing reasons:

1. Not enough Christians know Muslims or have Muslims as friends

2. Christians have apocryphal eschatology about the return of Jesus and end times that tends to otherize Muslims

3. Christians are not being sincere in their duty to love even their enemies (Emir-Stein Center)

When I spoke to him, he was quite forthcoming and welcoming. He said we disagree theologically, but we can be friends. He told me his views of Muslims changed over time, and his faith in Christ calls him to love and respect Muslims. He hopes to continue engaging with Muslims and build on that engagement to affect change for the betterment of our country.

In religious discourse in America, it is common to talk about a Judeo-Christian tradition (Leoffler). Jews and Christians share the same prophets, holy scriptures, and creation stories. The Christian *Bible*, for the most part, includes the Jewish scriptures, referred to as the Old Testament, and the Christian scriptures, which include the Gospels, the letters of Paul, and the Book of Revelation, commonly referred to as the New Testament. The Patriarch Abraham is commonly referenced in both traditions for his covenant with God and as the father of Isaac, his son Jacob, and the twelve tribes, of which Jesus is descended. However, conspicuously missing from this narrative is the detail that Abraham had another son in addition to Isaac. Before Isaac was born, Ishmael was his oldest son. He too was promised a great nation (BibleRef).

The Arabs claim descent from Ishmael. Prophet Muhammad considered Abraham as his father and Moses and Jesus as his brothers (Elias) (Deuteronomy 18:18). When the Muslim armies burst out of the Arabian Peninsula in the mid-seventh century CE, they conquered lands dominated by Christians such as Syria, Palestine, Iraq, and Egypt. In early Christian literature, on these Arab conquerors and the new religion they carried, Islam was considered a Christian heresy (OCIC). Christendom, for the most part, has not been able to come to terms with this familiar yet strange new faith.

Historically, Islam was not only a physical threat to Christian holdings in the Middle East and beyond, but it was an ideological competitor as well. For example, Christianity can easily distinguish itself from Buddhism and Hinduism. Their originations, scriptures, peoples, and concepts of God are sufficiently different and detached enough to allow Christian proselytizers to dismiss them as a threat to the unique message of salvation and redemption through the sacrificial death of Jesus. Islam, however, presents a direct challenge to the Christian narrative and its authority because it coopts the Judeo-Christian narrative and proclaims it as its own.

Muslims consider Abraham as one of the greatest of God's prophets, and through Ishmael, also inheritors of his covenant with God. Islam adopts all of the Jewish and Christian prophets, acknowledges the same God of the Jewish scriptures and considers the Torah and Gospels as divinely revealed books that have been corrupted over time, and that the *Qur'an* came as a final revelation to mankind to correct, clarify, and guard over previously revealed scriptures. Therefore, Muslims believe God is the Creator of the heavens and the earth, and Adam. More than this, Islam views all the previous prophets as Muslims because the word Islam connotes "submission." In this instance, submission to the one true God, Allah. Therefore, from Adam to Jesus are considered Muslims because they submitted their will to the will of God.

On the face of it, it appears as if the two faiths have a lot in common, and they do. It is precisely these commonalities—especially the belief in one Omnipotent Being who created everything and commands mankind to do good and adhere to His will, or face the consequences—that Muslims and Christians in America should ultimately and mutually embrace, come to common terms with, and ally together against other shared challenges. However, the devil is in the historical details.

In Western Christendom, there is this view that the Muslims stole Jerusalem from the Christians in 638 CE. Today, some Christian revisionists find justification for the Crusades of the Middle Ages under the pretext that the land of Palestine where Jesus came from had been Christian lands. However, they miss the point. Palestine was occupied by Ancient Rome long before the rise of Christianity. The way the Holy Land became a part of Christendom was by virtue of Rome adopting Christianity as the religion of the empire upon the conversion of Constantine to Christianity around 313 CE.

In fact, the Bedouin Arabs have lived as nomads throughout the Middle East as far back as 3000 BCE. Some of them converted to Christianity and, later, the vast majority became Muslims. Logically, the indigenous people of the region had more claims to the land than Greeks, Romans, or other Europeans. In addition, not many appreciate the intricate relationship between the various peoples of the Holy Land. The Prophet Moses, who freed the Children of Israel from bondage, led them to the Promised Land and gave them the Torah, and God's law was married to a Midianite woman, Zipporah, an Arab (Baxter). This means the descendants of Moses are half Arab (ESL Connexus).

Muslim rule over the Holy Land has been the longest and most stable, about twelve hundred years (Grabar). However, more than physical control over territory, Islam has been a civilizational and religious competitor to the Judeo-Christian tradition. The Islamic empire is recognized for its advancements in the fields of science, architecture, medicine, law, and economics. A burgeoning Europe built upon this legacy of Muslim advances in these areas and relied on it during the renaissance period and, later, the industrial revolution and the rise of Western European colonialism. Due to the upheaval of the European Dark Ages, Muslim scholars studied, translated, and preserved Ancient Greek and Roman texts that were later rediscovered by the West (Adamson).

On the religious level, Islam presented a threat as well. It appears as if Islam perfected the Judeo-Christian religious tradition in a permanent way. A comparison of the religious scriptures is instructive. The *Bible* is a religious text believed by many Christians to be divinely inspired. Its books are believed to have been compiled over a two-thousand-year period from the time of Moses to the Gospel authors of the first Christian century, between 60 to 95 CE. There are over forty different writers, some of them known, some unknown. The *Bible* is divided between various developments of Hebrew and Greek, yet Jesus almost certainly spoke Aramaic, which is a Semitic language close to Arabic and Hebrew common in the area where he lived in first century Palestine.

In comparison, the *Qur'an* is one book that is about one-fifth of the Christian *Bible*. Written down and memorized over a period of about twenty-three years, in one language—Arabic—by one author considered to be God. Apart from this background, what is interesting about a comparison of the two texts is that the *Qur'an* somehow refines, improves on, and simplifies the *Bible*. Prophets in the *Bible* are prone to sin, adultery, murder, and idol worship. The Qur'anic stories of these same prophets sheds the baggage of the biblical narrative and replaces it with purer stories and circumstances. Jewish and Christian theologians like to portray the failings of the biblical prophets as a demonstration of their humanity.

It's not that human beings are not susceptible to sin.

However, the Prophet Muhammad, a fallible human being, is considered sinless in conveying the message he was sent to deliver. It doesn't make sense that divinely inspired individuals of God would commit the very sins they came to preach against and eliminate. Why would people believe a liar, accept warnings against adultery from an adulterer, or give up worship of idols based on the preaching of an idolater? It's not that hard of a concept to imagine. I personally know many people who are obviously not prophets and not sinless, but who are also not liars, adulterers, murders, or idolaters.

Interestingly, what the *Qur'an* leaves out is amazing. The flood story of Noah, memorialized in film, is mentioned in the *Qur'an* as well as the *Bible*. However, the Qur'anic narration conspicuously leaves out that it was the entire world that was flooded as opposed to a section of the earth.

The word "day" in the *Qur'an* does not only mean a twenty-four-hour period. It also means an epoch or period of time thereby harmonizing the creation story of six days with modern scientific information indicating billions of years for the formation of the earth. It also denies that God needs, or rested, on the seventh day.

The *Qur'an* also denies that Jesus was crucified or died on the cross. Like Christians, Muslims believe he was raised to heaven. Muslims believe Jesus is sinless, he is the Messiah, he was born of the Virgin Mary, he cured the blind, the leper, and raised individuals from the dead but by God's permission. In addition, it denies the divinity of Jesus and condemns the belief in the trinity. Islam espouses a simple unity of God as opposed to a complex unity as claimed by Pauline Christianity.

When it comes to religion, Christianity has nothing on Islam. Both faiths call humanity to what is laudable and good such as implementing justice, loving thy neighbor, feeding the hungry, helping the poor, uplifting the downtrodden, and so forth. However, a more in-depth comparison of the *Qur'an* and *Bible* uncovers additional differences.

An objective examination of violence in the two holy scriptures elicits surprising results. The *Qur'an* refers to warfare, however, in treating the verses in context, historical circumstances, and linguistically one can fairly conclude that in Islam, engaging in warfare is a defensive position, not much unlike just war theory in Catholicism. When explicit commands to kill the unbelievers appear in the *Qur'an*, it is patently clear that such a directive is in the context of the heat of battle. When opposing armies face each other in an imminent locking of arms, it's kill or be killed. Yet, the word sword is not mentioned once in the *Qur'an*. In addition, whether one agrees with the Muslim position or not, the Muslim narrative is that Muhammad peacefully preached his message to the pagan Arab tribes. It is the response of the Meccans who intended and acted to eradicate Muhammad and his followers that caused the Muslims to defend themselves so that they would not be wiped out of existence. The nascent Muslim community defended against an existential threat. Muhammad overcame his enemies in this world, unlike a crucified Christ.

Violence in the Biblical context, especially the Old Testament, is bloodier and more replete. In battling the Midianites, Moses commands the men, infants, and women who have known men be put to the sword. The virgins were to be left alive and kept as concubines (Numbers 31). Joshua, the successor to Moses, was instructed by God to kill every living thing in the City of Jericho, including the livestock (Joshua 6:21).

In the Old Testament, God orders the Israelites to kill all of the Amalekites including the women and children (1 Samuel 15:3).

The point is either one accepts for both the historical context of the times, the justification of self-defense or concedes the *Bible* contains more references to violence than the *Qur'an*. The ideal is to accept the good each has to offer without having to demonize the other.

Even though Christians will fervently distinguish God's progressive nature from the Old to the New Testament, one still finds violence in the New Testament as well. When Jesus returns, he will order those who did not believe in him to be brought before him as a footstool to be slayed (Luke 19:27).

Some Christians feel unrestrained in their criticisms of Islam and its treatment of women, but the *Bible* does not fair better on this score either. Women are poorly depicted throughout the *Bible*. Eve caused Adam to eat of the forbidden fruit tree (Genesis 2:4-3:24). Child bearing is a punishment for women (Genesis 3:16). A woman who dishonors her father's household is to be put to death, a clear reference to honor killing

(Deuteronomy 22:21). In the New Testament, Paul writes that women are to be quiet in the church and are to be subservient to the man (1 Timothy 2:12).

In this context, the attack on Prophet Muhammed and his marriage to Aisha at nine years of age is way off base and unjustified. Let's first dismiss the fact that fourteen hundred years ago in the Arabian Peninsula that was an accepted practice, as it was in other parts of the world. Let's also ignore that such marriages were not consummated until the girl reached the age of puberty and was capable of bearing children. Let us also gloss over that females in the desert matured earlier than girls of today. Let us conspicuously ignore the narration in the *Bible* that suggests Joseph may have been an old man when he was wedded to the Virgin Mary who, according to Jewish custom, would've been in her early to mid-teens.

Orientalists who study Islam and are very critical of the faith never criticized the Prophet's marriage to Aisha as one of the attacks on Islam until the twentieth century. It is a modern criticism. What is interesting is that only recently have American states raised the legal marriage age to avoid accusations of pedophilia and statutory rape. Also, for those voices so keen on liberating the oppressed Muslim women, did they inquire how Aisha felt, what she said about her marriage and husband and the full and liberated life that she lived? She was a scholar, she appeared on the battlefield and she praised her life with the Prophet Muhammad.

The problem, therefore, is not just that we are applying contemporary moral standards through a Western, liberal, and feminist lens on the past, we are also confused about the definition of marriage, causes of pedophilia, appropriateness of gender identity, and moral limits of sexual expression. As the dominant society in the world, we judge traditional societies based on our own fluctuating norms and move the goal post at will. This confusion and double standard apply to other aspects of the human condition when it comes to Muslims and Christians in the west.

When we put people to death, it's justified, when Muslims do so, it's barbaric and unjustified. Westerners are quick to point out that in Islam you can be put to death for apostasy, leaving the faith. This is not entirely accurate. This issue, like any other, has to be discussed in context. In a Western society where there is a division of church and state, only a person who engages in state treason can be executed. In Islam, where the line between church and state is erased, treason is defined differently. Death as a punishment for apostasy does not exist in the *Qur'an*, but is clearly mandated in the *Bible* (Deuteronomy 13:1-12). To the contrary, numerous verses in the *Qur'an* enshrine and support choice in belief. Apostasy in Islam is tied to treason against the nation of believers, and it includes actions that are seen as subversive and meant to destabilize society.

Obviously, secularists and atheists may criticize both Christianity and Islam on these issues. However, it is disturbing to Muslims when such criticisms come from Christians as if they have not read their own scriptures or censored their own beliefs. Christianity as a faith has nothing over Islam. Salvation in mainstream Christian theology requires a blood sacrifice and is linked to original sin, which are two concepts rejected in Islam.

In mainstream Christian theology, salvation is achieved through the belief and acceptance of a crucified Christ who died for the sins of humanity. Original sin is key to understanding salvation and the role of Jesus. While the *Qur'an* narrates a similar story regarding Adam and Eve, it omits original sin. In Islam, when you commit a sin, you do not confess to a priest or take heart in the knowledge that God shed His own blood and died to wipe out that sin you had just committed. In Islam, you turn to God in sincere repentance, refrain from again committing the sin, and seek God's forgiveness, and He will forgive you.

The Jesus in the *Qur'an* is different from the Jesus depicted in the Gospels. Although it must be said that the rendering of Jesus in the *Bible* does not make the concept of trinity easy to grasp or believe. Jesus said "The Father is Greater than I, of my own will I can do nothing without the father" (John 14:28). When he went into the garden of gethsemane, he prostrated to the ground on his face and he prayed to the Father. Muslims still pray this way. It is also mentioned that Abraham and Moses put their faces to the ground in prostration. Rarely do you find Jews and Christians praying in this way.

Christians and Muslims believe in the same God, but Christians visualize a trinitarian God. One God, three persons. Apart from the contradiction of three in one is the egotism of belittling God to the point where our arrogance relegates Him to coming down on Earth in the form of a human being, suffering and dying for us because He loved us so much. This is not to say that God cannot do what He wills or that God is not all loving. It seems as if we created this god to satisfy our egos and console ourselves. While no good Christian uses this understanding of salvation to commit sin, in theory, it is a license to sin because the offense has already been paid for. God created us knowing our faults, therefore, He can forgive without the need for blood.

The list of these differences goes on and on. I chose to illustrate these differences not to alienate Christians but as a way of responding to the hypocrisy exhibited by Christian Islamophobes. In addition, I have chosen to characterize Christian-Muslim relations in America in this way to come to common terms and an understanding.

Muslims and Christians both believe in the same God, have a lot in common, can be friends while differing on theology, and can come together to change America for the better.

People of faith have done so much good in the world. Muslims and Christians can do so much good in America when it comes to bringing about social justice, narrowing the economic disparity in society, stamping out racism, and preventing wars of aggression. They also have a cause to stem the growing tide of atheism.

The problem with modern atheism is not denying the existence of God. This is clearly a human prerogative. The *Qur'an* basically states whoever so wills believe and whoever so wills disbelieve. The issue is the attack on religion and people of faith. Some atheists blame society's problems on religion and people of faith. If religion is manmade as some claim, why should I accept another human being's outlook about the world? One says God exists, one says no. I don't see how believing in the unseen makes one prone to be a worse person than one who only "believes" in what one can observe or "know."

If I had the liberty to choose, I would choose to benefit from both the *Bible* and the *Qur'an*. I would seek to forge meaningful relationships with Christians who share similar conservative views.

For Christians in the US, Islam's challenge for them is how can they build bridges of engagement on shared concerns such as morality in our lives, foreign wars, preservation of life, and electing people of faith and principles to elected office.

CHAPTER 8

Terror Rehab

"Generally speaking, punishment makes men hard and cold; it concentrates; it sharpens the feeling of alienation; it strengthens the power of resistance"
—FRIEDRICH NIETZSCHE, ON THE
GENEALOGY OF MORALS / ECCE HOMO

Growing up, I never thought I would be a lawyer, much less one representing clients accused of terrorism. It took a massacre and a custom-made T-shirt to change the trajectory of my life.

I was nearly sixteen years old in the summer of 1982. I remember watching the Israeli invasion of Lebanon that resulted in at least fifteen thousand civilian deaths and the ensuing Sabra and Shatila massacre on television that September (Ross). The gruesome killings of nearly three thousand Palestinian refugees by Lebanese Phalange militiamen in the squalid refugee camps of Beirut made major headlines around the world (Fisk) (Fisk) (Shakra). In identity politics, it was the Palestinians' 9/11. For me, it was a crash course in the First Amendment.

Spurred to action, I had a T-shirt made that said "Long Live Palestine" on the front and "P.L.O." on the back. It didn't matter at the time that I had very little knowledge of the Palestine Liberation Organization and Yasser Arafat's quest for a Palestinian state.

I must've worn it two or three times before it got noticed. I was walking in the hallways with one of my friends when I heard the theatre teacher, Mr. Burke, bellow out to another colleague, "I don't care what anyone says I'm going to get that shirt off his back."

My friend Jim said, "Whoa! Did you hear what he said? You are going to be in trouble."

I was startled by the teacher's reaction. The incident lingered with me throughout the day.

Before dismissal, I got called out of class to see the principal. I had never been in trouble with the principal before, but I went to his office with the bravest face I could conjure up. Mr. Gerald Gallagher was middle aged, tall, and Irish. He sat me down in his office and after some introductions of how I was doing in school and why I was being called into his office he said, "Ashraf, you can't wear this shirt to school anymore. I know that it means a lot to you but I am responsible for the security of the school including your safety."

I was incredulous and managed to muster the courage to ask, "Why can't I? I see other students with all kinds of shirts. It doesn't have any swear words or anything."

He looked at me with what seemed to be some empathy and said in a more subdued tone, "I know the Palestinians have a cause. I'm Irish and the Catholics have been fighting for freedom for a long time. You and I know what these letters stand for but I can't have this shirt misconstrued as gang colors or signs. I am responsible for the safety of everyone, including you." He could tell I was severely disappointed and he added, "Do you understand? If you come back with this shirt, you will be sent home and you won't be able to come back if you wear it again."

I left his office dejected. I went back to my homeroom, and I told my homeroom teacher what had happened. Mr. Cortesi, Italian and Catholic, was witty, kind, and truly cared about his students.

When we were together alone even then he whispered, "I'm going to tell you something and if you tell anyone you heard it from me, I will deny it."

My ears perked up. I knew if he was so adamant about this it was important. "There is an organization called the American Civil Liberties Union, the ACLU. They defend peoples' rights. You have a right to wear that shirt. It's political expression."

"How do I contact them?" I asked with my eyes wide opened.

"Look them up in the telephone directory. They probably have an office downtown. Have your parents call them." *Have my parents call them?* I thought. I was so grateful for the hope that he gave me even though I was not sure where this would end up. Intuitively, I knew getting my parents on board was going to be an uphill battle.

As soon as I got home that day, I pled my case to my mother. She was at home cooking Mulukhiyah (a jute leaf in the Mallow family) with meat and rice. I told her what had happened. She was very sympathetic, but this was beyond her control to deal with. "Tell your father when he gets home."

My father was a foreman at Schwinn Bicycle Company. When he got home that day, I barely gave him time to settle in.

"Dad, the principal told me I can't wear this shirt. One of the Jewish teachers at school was yelling about me. It's Palestine…"

My father said, "You have to do better in school. We don't want trouble. I'm not up for this."

At this point I was fighting back tears.

"You told us we were Palestinians. You said we have to fight for what we believe in. How could you let them do this to me? It's not right. All you have to do is call the ACLU!"

It took days to convince him, but my father relented and called the ACLU.

We were given an appointment to meet with attorney Barbara Bandes. She asked us questions, said the ACLU would take our case, and that I had a First Amendment right to wear my shirt as it was freedom of speech and political expression. She said that if we were contacted by journalists, they would handle all media calls. I was proud of my father for standing by me.

The weeks passed, and what I distinctly remember was receiving a series of letters between the ACLU and the Chicago Board of Education. No litigation was had because the Board backed down and acknowledged that I had a right to wear the shirt. I couldn't believe the outcome. I was so happy. I just kept wearing that shirt to school until I don't know what happened to it.

One day, I was walking down the stairs and up came the principal in a hurry skipping a couple of steps at a time. When he saw me, he said, "Good for you, Ashraf," and he gave me a thumbs up as he whizzed past me.

This exercise in freedom of expression impacted my life greatly. It taught me that one has to stand up for what one believes in, rights have to be defended and fought for, and a just cause cannot prevail on its own. It needs backers. The incident is the main reason I ended up becoming an attorney.

Twenty years on, the US reaction post 9/11 has been a stain on America's reputation for freedom and justice. In addition to the unjustified wars on Afghanistan and Iraq, post 9/11 "terrorism" prosecutions were overbroad, discriminatory, and in some instances down right corrupt (Lu). Over six trillion dollars, nearly a million dead, and twenty years later, the "war on terror" continues (Kimball).

I can still recall those tense moments on 9/11 that turned into hours, then days, then weeks, and then years. Yes, we had been attacked, but to be just, we had to act with our brains not our brawn. The Muslim community was unknown, thus vulnerable. I was determined that in America everyone had a right to be represented. So, after I started my own solo practice, I was free to take on the cases of my choosing.

It was Friday, June 27, 2003. My colleague, Ismail (Randall) Royer, had been working at my law firm as a paralegal and researcher for just a few short weeks. We had been friends for a few years, and we both performed the pilgrimage to Mecca together in 2000. Ismail was a white American man from St. Louis, Missouri, who converted to Islam at age nineteen. He was bright, idealistic, and sure of himself. I believe precisely because of this the FBI and the prosecutor's office targeted him for investigation in a case that came to be known as the "Virginia 11" and the "Virginia Jihad Network."

They couldn't understand why a young, intelligent, educated white male would convert to Islam, and treated him as if he was a traitor to his country. It didn't matter that otherwise he was a good American, he believed in the same God as they did, he was leading a good wholesome life, or, most importantly, he neither intended to nor attacked his country.

By this time, it became clear to Ismail that the FBI was going to arrest him even though it was not clear what crimes he and the others may have committed. He trusted me with his plans.

"I want to hold a press conference and tell my side of the story. I will take care of the logistics and the program. I would like you to be there as a lawyer and family friend."

I said, "You can count on me. Just let me know the time and place."

After all, if he was up for it, so was I.

Although embroiled in his own developing case, stemming from the US Attorney's Office in the Eastern District of Virginia (EDVA), Royer was passionate about helping others, and developing a public relations campaign for Rabih Haddad, one of my clients at the time.

Rabih Haddad, a Lebanese Christian convert to Islam devoted his career in the humanitarian field serving those less fortunate. As a cofounder of the Global Relief Foundation (GRF), he was targeted by the US government because of his immigration status. After 9/11, in a government sweep reminiscent of the Palmer raids of the 1920s, immigration officials rounded up several hundred Muslims and placed them in secret deportation proceedings (Associated Press in New York). I was forced to represent Rabih in hearings that were closed to the public after 9/11. This did not sit well with Prof. David Cole of Georgetown University, who along with the ACLU and a private firm brought me on board to file a lawsuit against the government to open up Rabih's hearings. In *Detroit Free Press v. Ashcroft*, the Sixth Circuit

Court of Appeals upheld a lower court ruling opening the hearings to the public. In his opinion, the late Judge Daymon Keith famously said, "democracies die behind closed doors" (Kutler).

Although Rabih was eventually deported, freedom-loving Americans came together to stand for justice in his case. I recall reaching out to the late Congressman John Conyers' office to explain Rabih's case. He invited me to his congressional office.

He said, "Ashraf, I want to visit your client. What's being done to him is unjust."

Congressman Conyers had read Rabih's open letter in a local Michigan paper.

To: "Lady Liberty"

My Dear Sweet Lady:

You don't know me, yet I am one of your forsaken sons. In my dreams you come to me with promises of freedom and great aspirations, in a land far away.

"One nation, indivisible, under God," you said. "Life, liberty, and the pursuit of happiness were guaranteed to all," you said. "A land where justice is blind," you said. Your words swept me up in a tornado of hope, dreams, and inspiration. I answered your call and came to you with open arms, and oh, what a sight you were! Standing tall over the world, holding your

torch like a beacon, calling stray ships on a turbulent ocean to safe harbor.

It was then that I pledged to you that I will uphold and practice the values that you stand for. Little did I know that I will be persecuted in your name, and little did you know what your children were doing behind your back, some wittingly, but most unwittingly. They are afraid, my dear Lady, and fear almost always begets hate. I have done my best to preach and explain. I made every effort to promote and expedite healing among all of your children who are still anguishing and agonizing over the national tragedy of Sept. 11. I condemned and denounced those barbaric acts of horrific terrorism. I called upon your children to come together and embrace one another. I implored them to triumph over adversity and flock to your side in a show of unity and defiance to those who would rob us of the values that define our way of life.

Someone once said, "There is nothing as strong as real gentleness, nothing as gentle as real strength." When I think of this, I think if you! Take a look over your shoulder and whisper gently to your children not to be afraid. From my jail cell, and because of my faith and trust in Almighty God, I tell you that my spirit is free! Free as the meadowlarks of Nebraska, proud as the bold eagles of Alaska. You do not have to worry about me; just keep your torch burning high, and remain in the dreams of the oppressed and persecuted around the world. Continue to be the beacon of hope and oasis of prosperity for so many.

Come what may, I will hold true to the pledge I made to you, "truth" and "justice" will ultimately prevail!

With love and hope,

Your forsaken son,

Rabih Haddad

Monroe County Detention Center

Rabih was humbled by the gesture of a well-respected elected official visiting him. Conyers told him, "Rabih, I apologize for what you are going through. Our nation has a history of oppression. It's our collective duty to stand up for what's right. I can't guarantee an outcome but we will open up your hearings and give you a fair chance."

Rabih said, "Congressman Conyers, I am humbled that you would come to visit me in this place. It has been difficult on me, especially because of my family."

"You hang in there. The community is with you, and my office will coordinate with Ashraf," he said.

Meanwhile Ismail, true to his advocacy training, strong writing skills, and deft public relations acumen, put his talent to work in developing a PR campaign for Rabih. Ismail had worked as a case manager at the Council on American Islamic Relations (CAIR) and had gone to Bosnia. He fought to protect Bosnians from ethnic cleansing.

Ismail had planned a press conference that June day at the National Press Club, and I was to participate, to point out the governmental harassment. The FBI had been questioning

Royer upon his return from Bosnia shortly after September 11. In the brewing government indictment, there was no claim of attacks on the US, just some vague laws and statutes that mandated Royer would end up receiving a twenty-year sentence.

His arrest was frightening.

It was clear that we were being monitored by the government. The intended press conference had forced the government's hand. He and six others were arrested in the early hours of that Friday morning. Despite the government intimidation, I resolved to attend the press conference and raise the voice of the voiceless. After our press conference, the media headed over to the Department of Justice who announced a press conference to market the success of its terror prosecutions (Meyer).

I thought I would be arrested that day for having the nerve to go ahead with the press conference when it was obvious that the arrests were timed to derail Ismail's plans to expose the government's targeting of him and his paintball friends.

At his sentencing on April 9, 2004, Ismail wrote a thirty-page letter to Judge Brinkema taking responsibility for his actions, detailing aspects of his life, and demonstrating his opposition to extremism (Royer). He was sentenced to twenty years in prison. He was released in 2017.

These cases are but a few of the stories I have been involved in or are familiar with over the years. If one read the news reports at the time, one would think terror was lurking behind every door and our government was like a fanaticized super hero ready, willing, and able to save America from the Muslim threat.

I have known, represented, and assisted hundreds of Muslims caught up in politically motivated prosecutions and immigration proceedings. I worked with an array of prominent criminal defense attorneys such as Stanley L. Cohen, Michael Kennedy, Abdeen Jabbara, Lynn Stewart, Ron Kuby, and William Kunstler. William Kunstler was the well-known criminal defense attorney of the "Chicago Seven" charged with rioting and conspiracy at the 1968 Democratic convention. I interned for Kunstler and Kuby in the summer of 1994, while he was writing his book *The Life of a Radical Lawyer*. Because I called him Mr. Kunstler instead of Bill, like everyone else, he would jokingly say, "See the Muslim shows me the most respect."

The attorney who stands out most for me, though, is the former Attorney General of the United States Ramsey Clark.

I met him many years ago at a Muslim convention in the mid-nineties. I interviewed him then on why he would represent individuals charged with terrorism. His response was "Everyone deserves a defense." About twenty years later, I had the distinct privilege to sit down with him and discuss our mutual client Sh. Omar Abdulrahman. In the media, he was portrayed as "the blind Sheikh." He gave me advice on how to handle the case and wished me luck.

Ramsey Clark, who I interviewed for this book at ninety-three years old, was the oldest living Attorney General of the United States. He passed away on April 9, 2021. His father, Supreme Court justice Tom C. Clark, who also served as Attorney General of the US in the late forties, resigned from the Supreme Court so that Ramsey could assume the position of Attorney General and avoid a conflict of interest. He was appointed as the sixty-sixth Attorney General of the United States in March 1967.

When I sat with Mr. Clark in his Manhattan home to discuss the case and other matters, I asked him about his opposition to the Iraq war and the assassination of the Kennedy brothers. I talked to him again for this book. While he was less involved in worldly affairs, he still read the newspaper daily, and he had a keen sense of where our country currently stands.

"We are in trouble," he told me.

I wanted him to know that a lot of the convicted Muslims who served long sentences were released and did well on the outside. He was happy to hear it.

"I am glad of that. A lot of people were wronged," he said.

I followed the Virginia cases closely because I knew some of the men personally. Nineteen years later, every one of the men charged in the "Virginia 11" has been released. Like most Muslim defendants I have come across, they were all targets of an overzealous prosecution in targeting Muslims after 9/11. One prosecutor said all Muslims lie. Another prosecutor hid exculpatory evidence from the defense. FBI agents harassed the Muslim community by knocking on businesses in front of patients, clients, and customers. Prison guards physically abused detainees (Gerstein). As far as I know, all of them maintained their faith while in prison. All of them are rehabilitated. And all of the ones I spoke to for this book expressed good will toward the United States and its people. All criticism was toward individual prosecutors and agents and the failure of US foreign policy.

Every single person I know came out far better than what one would expect. They were all welcomed by their communities, they were assisted in assimilating back into society, they were provided jobs and financial assistance, and some were married. I asked all of them the following questions: (1) What was the most grievous violation in your case? (2) What was your faith able to do for you during your incarceration? (3) What do you wish for the United States? I am only including a couple of them as they are reflective of those I have spoken to with these questions. These were their responses:

ISMAIL (RANDALL) ROYER

Ismail saw the most grievous violation in his case was the overcharging of counts in his indictment to both force a plea bargain and the exploitation of such overreaching charges to justify the government's conduct after 9/11 in prosecuting these cases. He vehemently resented the government's devious attempts to link him to Al-Qaeda and terrorism in general. He felt it was way over the top for him to be facing a life sentence when no violence was involved.

Through his incarceration, he was able to discover deeper purposes of meaning as to what it meant to be a servant of

God. But for his faith, he would not have been able to deal with the stress, pressure, despair, and hardship of such long-term confinement. It allowed him to understand that his circumstances were not meaningless but had a reason and wisdom behind them. He even went as far as to say that the ordeal was a direct consequence of his action, in addition to being a test from God.

In the context of his ordeal, Ismail wants to see justice prevail in America. Despite the injustices he experienced, he insisted that justice was also on display in the criminal justice system. He felt a lot of goodness was on display as well from actors like Judge Brinkema in thoughtfully weighing the issues and the zealousness and professionalism with which his attorneys advocated and defended him. He hopes these exhibitions of justice continue to grow and overcome the injustices that exist. America has not collapsed and is still standing for a reason. Overall, the rule of law exists, and seeking, and believing in, justice is still the norm. He hopes America will increase in justice.

ABDURAHMAN ALAMOUDI
The biggest injustice, according to Abdurahman, in his case was the government focus and attempt to link him to terrorism. In essence, his charges amounted to accusations of tax and immigration fraud as well as prohibited travels to Libya. However, the government with malice intent portrayed Abdurahman as a terrorist sympathizer and enabler. He had served as a US Department of State ambassador of good will to the Muslim world. He believed in his role to show Muslims around the world that America is essentially

good and can be dealt with through understanding, dialogue, and good will. To have turned relatively minor violations of law into a twenty-three-year sentence was just unfair.

Maintaining his faith in prison was the key to his success and ultimate release. By keeping faith, he was able to continue to build up the inventory of good deeds necessary to earn him a high stature in the eyes of God, and in His presence, when he faces Him with an open book of all his deeds. He found solace in seeing other Muslims and helping them and others to cope with the harsh realities of prison life. He vowed on doing good deeds on the "inside" as he would have done on the outside. The consolation of knowing he had a purpose to do good was indispensable in not just surviving but thriving as well.

All his adult life has been spent in serving the Muslim community and positioning it to take its rightful place as an integral faith community positively contributing to the success of America. Although he does not dismiss the challenges and the injustices, he wants America to succeed as a free and just nation. It would be good for Muslims and all Americans. He does not subscribe to a clash of civilizations theory. He believes that through hard work and conscious thought, we can change the path of this nation. To that end, after leaving prison, he has embarked on a memoir to document his life and allow it to serve as a lesson and benefit to others who would seek to benefit society at large.

To the public, these men were terrorists. To those who know them, they were innocent and, in some cases, freedom fighters. They may have committed crimes but not crimes of terrorism. The fact that they came out of prison mostly intact and harbored no ill will spoke volumes of their fortitude and faith. They are doing well in society. They have shown that rehabilitation is possible.

Islam's challenge for America is to treat its incarcerated population with genuine rehabilitation in practice.

CHAPTER 9

Team Men and Women

"Surely the men who submit and the women who submit, the believing men and believing women, the obedient men and obedient women, the truthful men and truthful women, the patient men and patient women, the humble men and humble women, the charitable men and charitable women, the fasting men and fasting women, the men who guard their private parts and the women who do so, and the men who remember God often and the women who do so—for them God has prepared forgiveness and a great reward."

—QUR'AN 33:35

Let's embark on a little exercise together. Think for a moment. How did you come to have your current views on gender and the role men and women play in society? If you are a male, do you think of being a female, and vice versa, if you are a woman do you think of being a man?

What we derive from science is that men and women are more alike than they are different. This is important because

I do not question the equality of the sexes when it comes to intelligence, physical gratification, and spiritual needs.

The difference in anatomy, child-bearing capabilities, and temperament is where we find the most differences between men and women (Kaufman). Understanding this will help us come to the most appropriate way of viewing ourselves as sentient beings and allow us to complement one another rather than be at odds with one another.

So as not to be presumptuous or to speak unauthoritatively on behalf of the other gender, I will use my own personal experience as to how I arrived at my current views on gender issues. In the US, less than 10 percent of the population identifies as LGBT (Gates). Although important, I will not be addressing transgender and gender identification issues. I will be talking about women and men.

As long as I can remember, growing up in the seventies with two brothers, I formulated views of women based on what I observed of my mother and how males in my life treated women. As traditional Palestinian immigrants, the family setup was that my father worked outside to earn a living while my mother worked at home to nurture and care for the family. Growing up, my home dynamics seemed different from what I was observing of other children in school. Some came from dysfunctional or broken homes and some just led lives that were very different from my own. In school in the seventies and eighties, we weren't formally taught that men and women were equal. Compared to non-Western treatment of women, however, we practiced a more evolved form of equality in the US.

Women hadn't achieved the many gains we see today in terms of opportunity in the workplace, field of education, business world, and government. In practice, I personally experienced a degree of equality of the sexes. I assumed women were just as intelligent as men. Most women who wanted to work were able to do so—granted it was a different workforce then. Overall, women were making significant strides toward social equality. I grew up treating women without taking into consideration, not only the physical differences, but the established differing aspects of temperament between the sexes no matter how small.

Growing up with only two brothers did me no favors when I later interacted with females in my teenage years and when I married. I was conditioned not to take into consideration the obvious inherent differences between the sexes. In public interaction, I would treat a girl as if she was one of the guys. Today, that may be the desired behavior (i.e., that we don't differentiate between the sexes physically). I believe what we are all striving for is good overall moral behavior.

In terms of fairness, kindness, and honesty, as the verse above says, the genders are equal. However, not taking into account the need to discriminate for differences (in a positive sense) strained the relationship with my wife. When I decided to get married at the age of twenty-two, I opted for a traditional Palestinian girl from Jordan. Maybe, in hindsight, I was intimidated by the competitiveness of women in my own society. After all, I viewed the opposite sex as a potential partner. However, I did not want to marry a career woman.

The problem I encountered was that on one level I treated my "traditional" wife without taking into consideration her temperament, need for safety, financial security, and the qualities that made *her* feel like a woman, wife, and complete person. I was a product of my society, as she was a product of her society. I expected her to function in society like other women while maintaining traditional expectations, but I didn't empower her with the tools she needed to fully succeed. It was a big mistake on my part. I shirked my responsibility as a breadwinner. I expected her to work part time and take care of the household. I failed to act as a responsible partner to empower my friend of a lifetime. Only as I increased my knowledge and practice in Islam did I realize that men and women have a symbiotic relationship in marriage that Islam describes as a mutual garment covering of the other spouse. In addition, I realized that if I was honest, principled, respectful, diligent, and caring, I would find the same from my wife.

Today, sometimes, it feels like a war between the sexes. Some women view their disposition only as a result of an oppressive patriarchy. Seeking to redress this wrong, they go out of their way to compete and prove, whether to themselves or society, that they are just as smart and capable as any man. Insecure men and individuals in power who benefited from the "male" patriarchy feel threatened by female assertiveness.

The majority of society is caught in the middle of a contrived controversy. The problem is not male dominance per se, the problem is lack of moral, ethical, and spiritual principles among many in a secular society. Given that women and men worked together over the past couple of hundred thousand years to bring us to civilization (about six thousand years ago) and industrialization only a couple of hundred years ago, it's not a winning strategy to alienate each other in quest of an illusion of total equality. As it stands now, young males are skipping out on higher institutions of learning due to a perceived attack on masculinity (Halpin).

Who is the victim in this paradigm? The rest of society—men and women.

I chose to open this chapter with a verse of the *Qur'an* because I couldn't come up with anything more on point, reasonable, or that rings true when we talk about gender issues. The verse encompasses everything a human being, man or woman, should strive for in this fleeting life. True happiness stems from true faith, in this case, belief in the one unseen God who created us and authored the universe. Strong faith leads to conviction, conviction leads to action, good action is predicated on patience and evaluated by objective truths. The above verse encapsulates the characteristics required of all human beings. This will not satisfy everybody.

Gender issues are controversial for many reasons. There is a real historical gap in the opportunities afforded men and women. Due to modern technology, women have been freed from some of the obligations that have relegated them to a domestic status in the past.

Nothing has done more to divide the sexes in modern times, thereby weakening social cohesion, than the rapid push to bring about an equality of outcome between men and women. It's a bad idea. Men and women are equal in the sight of

God. Women and men are entitled to equality in dignity and respect. Women and men should have equal opportunity in contributing to a measurably healthy and stable society in such spheres as jobs, positions of influence, and power.

These views on gender issues are not limited to Muslims, people of faith, or conservatives.

Jordan Peterson, a clinical psychologist and academician-turned-motivator and influencer, has achieved growing popularity in the West with his book *Twelve Rules for Life* and his latest title *Beyond Order: 12 More Rules for Life*. Taped videos of his university lectures went viral on YouTube, and he has been a phenomenon in the West ever since. He is considered controversial in mostly liberal circles. He has become extremely popular with young men who feel alienated in today's society, in the sense that they don't feel motivated to take on responsibility and face the many challenges that society presents. He says it's desirable to work for equality of opportunity, but not equality of outcome.

Equality of opportunity means women and minorities should have the same opportunities as everyone else to obtain an education, get the job one desires, and have access to government and run for public office. Equality of outcome means we should basically work for a quota arrangement. Men make up about 93 percent of CEOs in the UK (Killian). In the US, women make up about 85 percent of elementary school teachers (National Center for Education Statistics). Since the population of men and women are about fifty/fifty, equality of outcome would necessitate that we have 50 percent female CEOs and 50 percent male elementary school teachers. This,

Jordan Peterson believes, is wrong and would not lead to desirable results.

He points to the outcome in the Scandinavian countries where the gender barrier is less prominent than any other society. Statistics show that when men and women are on equal footing and are allowed to choose their own careers, 90 percent of the healthcare field is made up of women, and men make up about 70 percent of engineers (Carroll). Peterson would say this is a result of the differences between men and women. Women are more inclined toward empathizing (social interaction), and the healthcare field more suits this temperament while men lean toward systematizing (more hands on) and therefore engineering is more desirable for them (Ramble).

Some factors are not taken into consideration when evaluating data salary gaps between men and women. This data does not take into consideration that men are more likely to work in jobs outside than women, and men are more likely to take dangerous jobs than women. Another reason is that making and inventing things leads to higher wages and earnings than say those who work in people-oriented fields. Whereas, you can quantify the projected profit earnings coming from say an iPhone or a multi-story building, it's more difficult to quantify the contribution to the profit margin coming from the human resources director. They are both obviously important, yet greed for maximum profit drives salary.

These factors taken into consideration further support the need to differentiate between equality of opportunity and equality of outcome.

Since Western neoliberalism insists there is no God, or at least there is no direct role for religion to play in the secular rule of law, it is up to man to determine his or her own destiny. It is up to man to decide what is right and wrong, who should be equal, and how they should be equal. The problem with this is that it presupposes that one group among others knows better, what is best for all human beings.

When people say everyone should be equal and have equal rights, what do they mean? For example, it seems like a no-brainer that women and men should earn equal pay. The statistics consistently show that men make more money than women. On the face of it, this seems to be unfair. No doubt, men and women doing the exact same job should earn the same wage, minus some egalitarian considerations encouraged in society.

For example, let's say a man and a woman both have the same job but the man is a bachelor and has no other financial responsibilities, whereas the woman is single and supporting four small children and her parents. Assuming equal pay, would it be acceptable for the man to voluntarily take less pay so the woman may get extra money to support her family? Or, without waiving his rights to equal pay, should the man be encouraged to donate a portion of his salary to provide assistance to the woman who is making the same salary but is financially unable to meet all of the basic necessities of her larger family?

The Qur'anic verse quoted encourages just that when it says "the men who give in charity and the women who give in charity…" While charity is encouraged in Western society, it is encouraged more in Muslim society as a Qur'anic directive. It is expected of those who have something to give and do their fair share. The ultrarich would be encouraged by religious principles of charity to give commensurately, without imposed legislation. In Islam, it is a communal obligation. All who can give are encouraged to give so the needs of the poor are met. In my opinion, implementing Islamic concepts of charity would better serve the American middle class than what we have now, where the gap in wealth between rich and poor is getting larger and larger. However, politicians are too busy raising and spending billions of dollars annually on promoting secular and political agendas.

Furthermore, a faith-based society can contribute to solving these wealth gaps that negatively impact the relations between the sexes. The divorce rate is high. Two-parent households make more money and overall lead to more successful and stable children (Collins). Some successful working women have decided, after achieving their career goals, they missed out on raising a family and spending less time in a stressful corporate environment, once attained, was not as fulfilling in the long run. For these women, some form of equality was obtained; however, it was at the expense of other needs.

Who says universal gender equality, as it is perceived or as it ultimately may end up, is right, desirable, or possible? More important than full equality of the sexes is working toward justice, respect, and dignity for all human beings. Where are the politicians on both sides of the aisle when it comes to putting human dignity for all into practice?

Even if the sexes earned the same, for example, if Congress was divided up evenly between women and men (or according to their percentages in society), and men and women equally shared the professions, would that eradicate poverty, greed, or oppression?

What will stop these vices and injustices are men and women working together with a common vision and goal in place. Religion has a positive role to play in achieving equity. Muslim women are doing their share.

Practicing Muslim women in America have probably done the most to portray a positive impression of Islam through their appearances and actions. Because of the head covering (hijab), Muslim women stand out more than Muslim men. When they accomplish something good for the society at large, it is important to recognize such achievements. These Muslim women provide a modern model of how one can be "religious" and successful in a secular society. They also differentiate between male abuse of power and males being the sole problem.

One such woman is Abrar Omeish. When it comes to glass ceilings, she shattered a few in Virginia and nationally. At age twenty-four, she was one of the youngest persons to ever hold an elected office in Virginia. By winning a position on the Fairfax County school board, she became the first Muslim women (tied with Ghazala Hashmi, who won a State Senate seat in the same election) to be elected in Virginia. She was the first hijab-wearing Muslim and the first Libyan-American to ever be elected nationally (Taylor).

In addition to these firsts, what really distinguishes her from most politicians is that her philosophy of being a public servant comes from her Islamic upbringing. She truly wants to represent all of her constituents, and she is willing to fight the hard battles to bring more justice to politics. She realizes that all people, regardless of their backgrounds, want the same things: fairness, to be treated with dignity and respect, and not to be cheated or lied to.

At twenty-six, she has matured and developed views. Early on, she thought feminism meant equality. Now, she is more concerned about the epistemology behind what it means to be a feminist. She values equity over equality and insists on being true to herself and her Muslim identity.

When I asked her about what the hijab means to her, she said "It forced me to embrace my Islam. In questioning, it made me stronger in my faith. People asked me questions about it. It has certainly earned me immediate attention in politics. It holds me accountable, and I don't see myself as different because of my hijab."

A graduate of Yale, her intellect is apparent.

Yet, she gives justice for Palestine as an example where her objectivity is questioned by those with inherent biases. Despite the challenges, she perseveres.

When asked where she sees herself in the next twenty years, as a public servant, she is confident about climbing higher and higher, maybe a magistrate judge position in DC.

Her view on America's future, fifty years from now, is one of hope seeking to bridge the gap and cover common ground. From talking to her, one senses a strong personal commitment to ethics, and morality in politics. As a hijab-wearing Muslim woman of African heritage, she doesn't view the patriarchy as the overarching enemy to overcome at this time.

Another example of the melding of religious life with secular markers of success and assimilation is the Hijabi rapper and poet artist, Mona Haydar. Her videos are shocking to Muslims and non-Muslims alike. They are shocking to some Muslims because she is outspoken and performative in ways uncharacteristic of their notions of a religious Muslim. Non-Muslims are surprised that a religious Muslim woman can be so secular and profane at the same time, as if she was a nun who flew over the cuckoo's nest.

When I spoke to her, I found that she makes a very good case for harmonizing religious and secular life. This is the way many Muslims view their faith. You can be religious and still be a natural part of secular society.

In asking her about her provocative videos, she related how she ended up shooting "Wrap My Hijab" while she was obviously pregnant. The impetus was intuitive. She had been volunteering at Standing Rock to protest the Pipeline. Her intention was to have her baby and lose weight—a stereotypical expectation of the entertainment industry. A woman came up to her. Mona was seven months pregnant. The woman put her hands on Mona's belly. Mona later found out she was a Lakota elder who had been at Standing Rock since the beginning of the protests. She told Mona, "Oh, look, you brought this medicine with you." This simple yet surreal encounter reformatted her hard drive, as she puts it:

I was going to have this standard body type that was going to be beautiful, pleasing, the most aesthetically acceptable for a hip-hop music video, and it was going to be my first, so I wanted to look my best. But she rewired my brain. This part of my life, the way I look right now, it's an important message to the world. Raising this next generation in the right way, with the right message and on the right path is the medicine that we all need. I went back home and I told my husband I need to fly to Detroit; I need to shoot this music video as soon as possible because I was doing things in a very colonial brainwashed way of needing my body to look a certain way in order for it to be acceptable for a music video. And it caused so much cognitive dissonance for people. You know she's pregnant, she's Muslim, she's a woman and she's doing hip hop. None of this really makes sense to people.

Mona Haydar considers herself a feminist. She is married and says, "I want my husband to be the best masculine version of himself."

No matter how you define feminism, in its terms and origins, it is a Western construct. In addition, it places heavy emphasis on the model that women have been historically oppressed by men. From its purely Western origins, it takes a combative stance on how to solve this problem.

Instead of competing with each other in what is normatively accepted as good in society, we tend to compete against each other in our attitudes and roles. Islam focuses on the rationale, comprehensive, and fair understanding of the relationship between men and women. This does not mean others do not in practice exhibit the natural relationship between the sexes. If they do, they happen to practice the correct concept, which Islam espouses. On the other hand, Muslims in practice may contradict the Islamic paradigm.

Women and men complement and complete each other. As human beings, they both share the definitions of what it means to be human compared to something else. Men and women are equal in the sight of God. Women and men share the same obligations of morality, honesty, and uprightness universally expected in society.

This balanced understanding of the relationship between women and men has greatly benefited Muslim women in Western societies. I interviewed many Muslim women for this chapter. The women I interviewed were all practicing Muslims who wore the hijab, or Muslim head covering, and were at minimum college educated. Although they had differing views on the meaning of feminism, and why women have been historically oppressed, they all shared similar views that men and women complement each other based on Islamic principles. This has made them conspicuously successful. One woman told me that by wearing a hijab, she has neutralized the opposite sex's tendency to evaluate women in the workplace based on physical differences. "When I cover that beauty, which is reserved for my husband, I force other men to evaluate me based on my mind and my abilities."

I am all for working for an ideal. Some feminists may believe that the human race will ultimately reach some kind of nebulous full equality between men and women. However, I am not convinced it is the right goal to strive for, given the differences between men and women. We may not have the complete studies to establish that the marital bonding of a man and a woman, based on a division of roles, is the core essence of the human family. However, when practiced sincerely, fairly, and correctly, it has proven to be a solid model for humanity.

CHAPTER 10

Organized Violence

"The West won the world not by the superiority of its ideas or values or religion [...] but rather by its superiority in applying organized violence. Westerners often forget this fact; non-Westerners never do."
—SAMUEL P. HUNTINGTON, THE CLASH OF CIVILIZATIONS AND THE REMAKING OF WORLD ORDER

When it comes to war and the use of violence, it would serve us well to remember this quote. If our ideas are truly superior, we are obligated to lead by example in avoiding war and curtailing violence. As it stands now, the United States is exerting force instead of diplomacy. This eschews our ability to evaluate the success of our vision for the world and assess the validity of our actions.

Even though the early Christians were pacifists, violence in the form of war went hand in hand with Christian love. For the theologians, salvation was more important than the life of the body (Wells). Just war theory continued to develop until modern times. Justification for war is divided into the morality of going to war and the morality of conducting the war. According to the Internet Encyclopedia of Philosophy, several conditions must be met to justify war including:

1. The cause must be just.

2. The proper authority must make the decision to go to war.

3. The groups going to war must have the right intention.

4. War must be undertaken only as a last resort.

5. The goal of the war must be a likely emergent peace.

6. The war must be proportionate, that is, the good must outweigh the evil of a just war.

Even if the war is just, certain conditions have to be met as to how to conduct the war. These include:

1. Immunity of civilians.

2. Intended target versus unintended.

3. Proportionality regarding specific acts within war. All the above conditions have to be met for a war to be justified.

How do American wars in the past fifty years fare under such stringent conditions?

Let's take the ongoing war against Iraq. Was it a just war to begin with? Iraq hadn't attacked us. In cases of imminent hostilities from a belligerent, a preemptive strike is justification against an aggressor, according to some scholars. Was this condition met, given Iraq had no plans to attack us? We were told of weapons of mass destruction. There were none.

How about the proper authority making the decision to go to war? The UN Security Council did not authorize the invasion of Iraq in 2003. Even if America decided to go to war on its own, the Bush administration was in violation of the US Constitution by sidestepping Congress. Even though Congress "authorized the use of military force," it had not declared war since 1942 (History, Art & Archives: United States House of Representatives).

What was the intention of the United States and its "Coalition of the willing"? Was any of it a personal vendetta of the Bush dynasty? Did exploiting Iraqi oil have anything to do with the decision to go to war? Or, was it just a show of military might to establish American standing as the world's leading power (Butt)?

Since there doesn't seem to be any justifiable reason for going to war, it is moot to discuss what other options were available to avoid going to war in the first place.

How about the goal of peace as an emergent outcome? Even though President Biden intends to end "combat operations" at the end of 2021, there has been no peace in Iraq since the invasion. In 2020, the reported deaths of the war were close to one thousand (Hamourtziadou). The war has had an overall negative effect on the US, further detracting from the justness of the war. In addition to some 4,636 troops killed in Iraq, it is estimated that the US has spent over two trillion dollars to date (Cachero).

If this is not bad enough, at least two hundred thousand Iraqi civilians have been killed (Statista). This leads to another condition of how the war was conducted. Unfortunately, Abu Ghraib prison, Fallujah, Mahmudiya, and Haditha come to mind (Statista) (Aljazeera) (Schorr). These were different war crimes committed by our military. One of the most gruesome was the rape and killing of fourteen-year-old Abeer Al-Janabi and her family.

None of America's wars in the past fifty years fare any better in this analysis, least of which is Afghanistan. We left, after twenty years, with nothing but loss of life, capital, and good will. In these past fifty years, not only have Muslims been mostly on the receiving end, their countries have been occupied, bombed, or reduced to vassal states by America. In Islam, there is a similar just war theory (Parrott). Objectively speaking, Muslims have been able to adhere to their principles better than we have in the West.

In a survey tracking estimated death due to wars of the past two thousand years based on civilizational identification of seven civilizations, the Christian civilization has caused more deaths than any other civilization. The Islamic Civilization came second to last (bin Muhammad). Despite these findings, not only are Muslims most identified with terrorism, Islam is considered an exceptionally violent religion. Let's briefly look at Islam and violence.

The justifications for war are found in the *Qur'an*, the rigorously authenticated practice of the Prophet Muhammad—sunnah and hadith—and the jurisprudence of Muslim scholars. For brevity, and since the *Qur'an* is the main recipient of criticism about violence, we will focus on that. However, I am including a brief word on the Prophet Muhammad.

He is characterized as a warlord, especially when compared with Jesus Christ (peace be upon them both). There is a lot of misinformation and failure to contextualize him, his situation, and his times. Whether for good or ill, no one denies his profound impact on humanity until today. He was supremely successful as a religious figure and a "secular" statesman. Given the religiosity of the secular West, one assumes Westerners would view the Prophet Muhammad in a more favorable light. G. Bernard Shaw, the famous Irish playwright, critic, polemicist, and political activist, said of Muhammad: "I believe that if a man like him were to assume the dictatorship of the modern world he would succeed in solving its problems in a way that would bring it the much-needed peace and happiness."

The Qur'anic verses about warfare can be classified straightforwardly. The context is imperative. It is important, but irrelevant, whether non-Muslims accept the Muslim narrative in this context. What is controlling is that Muslims view the Prophet's mission as a defensive response to aggression. The mainstream classical narrative presents the context as follows.

Prophet Muhammad saw himself as a descendant of Abraham through his oldest son Ishmael. The children of Israel, descended from Isaac and his son Jacob—upon whom be peace—had already received many prophets. Muhammad began to preach at age forty in Mecca in 610 CE. He was living in a hub of trade for the Arabs who were pagan and prided themselves on their Arabic language. Although he and his small group of followers were boycotted, mocked, and physically assaulted, he peacefully preached in Mecca for thirteen years.

The leaders of Mecca, custodians for the pantheon of gods housed in the ka'ba, viewed Muhammad's message of one God as an existential threat to their standing. In 622 CE, he found safe refuge in a competing city state, later to be named Medina, where, with alliances with its Arab and Jewish tribes, he was accepted as the tutelar head of Medina.

Having escaped attempted murder, and now fearful that Muhammad and his followers would flourish, his tribe of Quraysh prepared to eradicate him and the new faith that threatened to supplant their rule and economy.

Only in this context did the Prophet receive revelation from God that he and his followers were allowed to take up arms to defend themselves against the existential threat posed by the Meccan army that had been assembled and planned to march on Medina.

The other verses that are often referred to by Islamophobes— and those they wish to mislead—give the command to kill the idolaters wherever they find them. This verse, in context, was simply the last stage of the war between Muhammad and the pagan tribes who had not accepted Islam and were still fighting the Muslim community. They were given four months to cease all hostility (Karim).

Similarly, all other verses refer to commands to kill the enemy while in the heat of battle, not as an aggressor. In addition, Muslims are commanded to pursue peace if the enemy inclines toward peace, even if their intention is a ruse or not sincere (*Qur'an* 8:61). When Muhammad triumphantly entered Mecca in 629 to 630 CE, he famously forgave his tribesmen in the fashion of the Prophet Joseph who said to his brothers, "No blame is on you, go for you are free today (Ahmed)."

Is it fair the Prophet Muhammad is vilified as a warlord in intellectual circles?

Jordan Peterson, the famous psychologist, admitted he had a problem with Islam because he couldn't understand it. He viewed Prophet Muhammad as a warlord, which is problematic for him. However, forty-three years ago, Michael Hart wrote a book *The 100: A ranking of the Most Influential Persons in History*. He ranked the Prophet Muhammad number one. He said, "My choice of Muhammad to lead the list of the world's most influential persons may surprise some readers and may be questioned by others, but he was the only man in history who was supremely successful on both the religious and secular level."

This is one of the reasons why Islamophobes stoke hatred against Islam and Muslims. They claim that Islam is a violent religion that mandates killing of non-Muslims. It is reprehensible to kill in the name of religion. This is a point that many in the West are unified on, and rightly so. However, it is equally reprehensible, and more so, to kill in the name of democracy, the free world, or American exceptionalism. Yet, that is exactly what is happening today throughout the world.

What is the justification to attack a country such as Iraq and devastate the civilian population, make unsubstantiated claims of ties to 9/11 and weapons of mass destruction, ignite a civil war and give birth to new and more dangerous enemies like the Islamic State? Although there is no justification, the answer is because we can. Al-Qaeda, the alleged perpetrators of 9/11, did not exist in Iraq until after we attacked and occupied that country.

What are we doing in the Middle East anyway?

The Arabs have roamed the Middle East, including the Eastern Mediterranean region for thousands of years and certainly before Rome or the Byzantines occupied those areas. Current Western and Middle Eastern relationships should be considered with this fact in mind. In other words, the Crusades of the Middle Ages were not justified attempts to reconquer lands lost by the Byzantines to the Muslim armies of the seventh century. Rome occupied the Middle East and later the Byzantine empire.

When US soldiers urinated on dead Taliban bodies in 2012, some of the rationale excusing this action was that some Taliban fighters had killed one or more of their comrades. This is ironic, given that we had invaded Afghanistan a decade earlier and killed thousands of innocent men, women, and children before this incident. The incident was also used as a justification of "if we don't kill them there in Afghanistan, they will kill us here in America." This is ironic, given that Afghanistan never attacked the US. More so, the Taliban who returned to power after a twenty-year debacle there had offered several options for resolving the issue of Osama bin Laden.

The US is not only misguided in its perceptions of Islam and its military entanglements in the Middle East and the Muslim world but it also provides cover for Israel to apply the same logic against the Palestinians. Americans are being lied to when Israel uses disproportionate force against rockets lobbed out of Gaza. Rarely is anyone killed from the thousands of homemade rockets while Israel kills thousands claiming self-defense. This is made to happen in a vacuum as if there was no occupation, inhumane blockade of Gaza, or restrictions on food, material, medical care, and travel imposed on two million unarmed civilians living in an open-air prison.

The West and Israel engage in the kind of racism that allows them to find justification for violently implementing their ideas for democracy, free markets, and exploitation of oil resources. When popular movements within the Muslim world react, they are labeled "terrorists." Take, for example, Palestine. The state of Israel occupied Gaza and the West Bank in 1967 and gradually began to illegally settle on that land while collectively punishing, pushing out, and killing the Palestinians.

Hamas was not established until 1987, after twenty years (or a generation) of brutal Israeli oppression and occupation.

"Suicide" bombings did not start until 1994, after a fanatical Jewish physician gunned down twenty-nine Muslim worshippers in the back while praying (Schweitzer).

Even though Hamas voluntarily stopped what are labeled as suicide bombings in the past several years, there has been no recognition of their ability to develop and change. When Hamas won legislative elections—insisted upon by the US—in 2006, the US, Europe, and Israel boycotted Hamas and blockaded Gaza. Such selectivity in implementing democracy becomes self-defeating.

Palestine, Iraq, and Afghanistan have something in common. A much weaker armed national force fought asymmetrically on their own land to kick out much more powerful military occupying forces.

It is ironic that Muslims "commit suicide" in these situations to free themselves of occupation while the greatest country on earth is losing tens of thousands of its own well-trained, heavily invested in, soldiers who end up committing suicide for mostly unknown reasons.

An estimated "30,177 active-duty personnel and veterans of the post 9/11 wars have died by suicide, significantly more than the 7,057 service members killed in post-9/11 war operations" (Suitt). We know they have PTSD, trauma, and difficulty assimilating back into society, but why would a freedom fighter promoting democracy and freedom end up killing himself?

I believe the answer is evident. They are taught a certain type of American exceptionalism that is deadly detrimental. We train our boys to be killers, we lie to them by telling them they are defending democracy, freedom, and their own homeland. Their experience of war tells them something different. When this racism leads to abuse, discrimination, rape, torture, and the murder of native people living on their respective lands, it doesn't sit well with the humanity of some of these soldiers. It's a simplistic answer; however, future studies will confirm the accuracy of this contention.

Islam came to solve such problems over fourteen hundred years ago. Just like billions of people have found solace, peace, and stability in Christianity and other faiths, so too have billions found salvation with Islam.

The West, with America at its helm, has embarked on a momentous journey and bid to lead in the world. We Americans have to ask the questions because we claim a representative democracy. Why do we want to lead? Who do we want to lead? What do we want to lead to, and why?

Islam offers a part of the solution to violence in the biblical story of Cain and Abel, which is also found in the *Qur'an*. The Qur'anic story focuses more on the subtle motives for the murder rather than the type of offering offered to God. Abel interestingly says to Cain, "As you are extending your hand with the intention of killing me, I am not extending my hand to kill you." What is equally interesting in this version is the next verse, which says, "Because of this we wrote upon the Children of Israel that whoever takes a life unjustly it is as if he has killed all of humanity and he who saves a life it is as if he has saved all of humanity."

Violence will exist as long as human beings exist because it is a potential manifestation of our nature and will. Thus, doing justice is the single most action those in power can take to minimize violence and the atmosphere that breeds violence.

CHAPTER 11

Food Is Medicine

"Let thy food be thy medicine and medicine be thy food."
—ATTRIBUTED TO HIPPOCRATES (400 BC)

From this quote, we have known for thousands of years that food and health are intricately related. One observation we have learned by now is the more we eat, the sicker we get. In addition, eating poor quality processed foods contributes to today's unhealthy lifestyles. Health is one of the most coveted conditions human beings seek.

In the US, we have unprecedented amounts of food, yet many Americans are deficient in basic nutrients, vitamins, and minerals, and what is synthetically being added to our food is making us sick. A combination of greed, the need for instant gratification, and apathy contributes to an unhealthy relationship with food. Manufacturers are producing food in labs warping the natural taste of food to sell their products. Americans who have been conditioned in a material society to demand a vast array of food regardless of supply and effect on the earth are overeating at alarming rates. In addition, even though we are generous in humanitarian giving, we can be indifferent to the food insecurity of those around us.

There is a saying of the Prophet Muhammad for which we should try to put into practice as much as possible:

A human being fills no worse vessel than his stomach. It is sufficient for a human being to eat a few mouthfuls to keep his spine straight. But if he must (fill it), then one third for food, one third for drink and one third for air (Sunan Ibn Majah 3349).

The takeaway of this wise saying is balance and moderation when it comes to food intake. In the West, food is everywhere and readily available. Obesity rates increased in the seventies (May). "Six in ten Americans live with at least one chronic disease, like heart disease, stroke, cancer, or diabetes. These and other chronic diseases are the leading causes of death and disability in America, and they are also a leading driver of healthcare costs" (CDC). It would be nearly pointless to rattle off the statistics of how unhealthy our food and eating habits are in America. The quality of the food and how much we eat and when we eat are key factors that determine overall health over a lifespan.

Nothing is wrong with making profits off of manufacturing food. However, greedy people are willing to sacrifice the environment and other people's health to increase profits. It's our fault if we allow ourselves to eat what's out there without being selective as to how the food is grown and processed.

After years of learning and experience with food nutrition, I make my own recipes for health. Here is a staple breakfast I have when I am not fasting.

Ingredients:

One to three eggs

Salt

Black pepper

Turmeric powder

Flax seeds (ground)

Sesame seeds (toasted)

Black seeds

Olive oil

Sumac

Boil the egg(s) for two to three minutes. Peel and add the rest of the ingredients to taste. Eat alone without bread. Each ingredient has a purpose that promotes a healthy body. Eggs are the embryos and food of once living creatures and are a natural source of nutrient-dense protein, fats, vitamins, and minerals (Gunnars). When reference is made to food items, I am referring to high quality, organic, and not processed where possible. Natural sea salt is not refined and contains trace minerals and electrolytes not found in common table salt.

Turmeric is a strong anti-inflammatory that is better absorbed with fat and pepper. Flax seeds contain omega-3 fatty acids that are beneficial for the heart, and it's a nutrient-dense food. It is said that during times of scarcity, the Roman Empire fed its military legions flax seeds. Sesame seeds are high in protein, vitamin B1, dietary fiber, and other nutrients and minerals. The black seed, listed by a US government website as a promising natural compound with potential benefits for COVID-19 prevention and cure, is a general immune booster that makes it an indispensable ingredient to any food (Badary).

Extra virgin olive oil is a high-quality monounsaturated fat that is caloric dense and contains antioxidants. Sumac is an anti-inflammatory spice with a tangy taste that complements the meal. Such a high protein breakfast keeps you satiated for longer and provides you with plenty of nutrients.

My perspective on food is based on Islamic teachings and the most up-to-date scientific knowledge. Eating the right foods, at the right time, in the right way, in the right amounts, is the difference between sickness and health.

In the *Qur'an*, there is a simple directive in the verse, "Eat from what is lawful and good (pure) on the earth." (2:168 & 172) Islam, for me, is in harmony with natural surroundings and scientific findings. If you treat your food like it's a potential cure, you will find enough food you like to keep you physically healthy. Eat natural, whole, and organic as much as possible. If you think you can't afford it, it's better to eat less good quality food than current amounts of unhealthy choices. Many social media influencers out there dedicate hours of content to healthy eating on a budget.

When we eat is also very important. Avoid eating at night, especially if it's your only meal of the day, and a large amount. Fast sixteen to eighteen hours a couple of days out of the week. The Prophet Muhammad fasted Mondays and Thursdays. When you break your fast, be selective in what you eat.

As advanced and effective as modern medicine is today, keep in mind that all medicine is derived from natural food, herbs, seeds, oils, plants, and so on. Although natural medicine is not as potent as its modern counterpart, it should be used as the default choice and first defense against combating disease and unhealthy conditions.

By the Middle Ages, Islamic medicine had developed to such an advanced degree that the Muslim physician and astronomer Ibn Sina's treatise on the human body, *The Canon of*

Medicine, was the essential reference book for Western medicine many centuries later (Encyclopedia.com). Ibn Sinna, known in the West as Avicenna, was a polymath and a pioneer in medicine and other fields. In addition to Muslim innovations in medicine, Muslim scientists benefited from Chinese and Indian philosophies and methods of health and healing.

Physical health is part and parcel of the overall health of the human being. How you eat, sleep, and move around daily will determine the quality of life you will lead.

FOODS TO KEEP AT HOME AND WHY

The idea that one type of food, herb, or spice can be a miracle cure for disease and modern conditions is of course not true, except that the black seed is a general immune booster that, if used correctly, can ward off disease before it takes hold. Supplements are a multibillion-dollar industry. I found the following foods, herbs, and spices are a must for my home: *Extra virgin olive oil, dates, raw honey, ginger, turmeric, thyme, basil, mint, raw apple cider vinegar, black seed, figs, olives, sesame seeds, flax seeds, garlic, lentils, organic meats and organs, ghee, raw nuts, whole grains, and raw dairy.*

The total rejection of grains by some health experts is misguided. Because of lectins, there is a campaign against such foods. We have been growing grains for thousands of years and they have served us well. The problem is the genetic modification, detrimental processing, and over consumption of grains, which is the cause of bad health, not the grain itself. Also keep in mind that cultures that consume these grains have more balanced diets and supplement their diets with offsetting ingredients that minimize the "bad effects." They soak grains overnight in water or whey to neutralize phytic acid and aid digestion. Fenugreek, which is commonly used in India and the Middle East, when consumed with carbohydrates like bread has been shown to regulate sugar therefore decreasing its spike on the glycemic index (Kumar).

Faith teaches one to curtail greed, respect the earth that God gave us as a trust, and ensure that the less fortunate of us are being fed and clothed properly. Today's market-driven society behooves us to have a faith-based lens in which to process information and respond in a way that avoids the pitfalls of greed, instant gratification, abuse of the environment, overeating, and apathy toward the less fortunate. This process begins with education.

ONLINE HEALTH INFLUENCERS

When you educate yourself on food and health, you must be a discerning consumer of information. One must realize that a lot of online content is redundant, confusing, and produced *en masse* for marketing purposes. One can benefit from the content by being educated and using common sense. I have been following two YouTube "food health experts" for years. Dr. Eric Berg and Thomas Deleuer promote a lot of products to drive their income. This is fine because if you are an educated consumer, you can use your best judgment to determine if something is right or necessary for you.

Both these influencers on YouTube promote the Keto diet. I have never gone on this diet, but I know it very well. I utilize the benefits and information derived from their content to implement the best eating habits and food consumption for me, and you should do the same.

Food is about moderation. Consider this, one-third of your stomach should be reserved for food, one-third for drink, and one-third for air.

This directive is powerful and can guide your life until the day you die. It makes complete sense. We know from studies that animals that are overfed get diseases and die earlier. Moreover, from experience, we know that overeating makes us sluggish, upsets our stomach, and so forth.

If you cannot fast, or even intermittently fast, try to keep this one rule. Only eat within a twelve-hour window as much as you can throughout your day. If you eat breakfast at eight o'clock in the morning, do not eat beyond eight o'clock in the evening. Just giving your digestive system that twelve-hour period to digest and relax from food can do wonders for you.

WHAT I'VE LEARNED

Eat whole foods from as natural or organic sources as possible.

Eat in moderate amounts and do not overeat.

Of the different diets out there such as keto, carnivore, paleo, and so on, I find the Mediterranean is the best.

One should be discerning and educated in considering any advertisement for health, or anything for that matter.

Marketed products are no more than hyped gimmicks of simple basic food products and eating habits. When people refer to certain supplements and ingredients, always keep in mind that the most natural state of that item is best for you in the long run. The whole natural form of that product in moderation is the best.

For example, when milk is referred to, do not think of milk purchased in the store or even organic milk, rather think of raw milk. The same thing applies to honey and olive oil. If I told you honey is natural and good for you, it would only be true if the nectar source was coming from wild flowers and not sugar. Olive oil is healthy. However, studies have shown that if it is not extra-virgin, it could have the opposite effect on one's health. In addition to consuming food in its most natural state, variety is important, and we must avoid extremes.

VEGAN CONTROVERSY
I am a firm believer that as God made us into nations and tribes, He also diversified our surroundings and access to food. Certain livestock, plants, and spices are native to one region in the world and not the other. The Muslim world has been privileged to be in the center of trade in the ancient world. Muslims had access to Indian spices and Chinese rice and tea.

It makes sense to eat food that is locally grown and native to the region. It is better to have a local apple from your backyard than to get an exotic fruit shipped over from Malaysia. Eating food such as fruits and vegetables that are in season is also a basic, sensible philosophy to adopt. We have to fight the urge to consume based on whims and desires without other considerations.

Many Hindus are vegetarian. It is a growing trend here in America. I respect that. Some people become vegetarian and vegan as a reaction to the ill treatment of animals in the food industry. I respect that as well. However, it does not mean vegetarianism and veganism are the best diets for human beings. Yes, a vegan can get enough protein to be a bodybuilder or strong man. However, that person is the exception. The best diet is a well-rounded diet that includes both animal protein in moderation and vegetable sources. In this regard, the "best" diet in the world is the Mediterranean diet. The region encompasses all the categories of natural and diverse food such as sheep, dairy products, olive oil, garlic, figs, vegetables, and fish.

RAW MILK CONTROVERSY

The prohibition against raw milk is no longer valid. The stated reason is to prevent outbreaks of bacterial contamination. That may have made sense a hundred years ago, however, today science will tell you that with safe handling, raw milk is superior to pasteurized and homogenized milk.

The real reason is because it is opposed by the conventional milk industry. It is just a fact that raw milk has natural enzymes and nutrients that are preserved and of benefit. When you heat milk (pasteurization) or over mix it (homogenization), you lose some of the benefits. Studies have shown that people who have allergic reactions, intolerance, and digestive issues with conventional dairy do not have the same problems with raw dairy.

When it comes to food, Islam teaches:

1. Eat what's pure and wholesome,

2. Eat in moderation, and

3. Share what you have with others who are less fortunate.

While many people practice these three teachings, not all of us practice them faithfully or consistently, and many people don't practice them at all. Just because we have access to all kinds of food at our disposal doesn't mean we have to follow the crowd. Islamic teachings of moderation and eating naturally are solutions to the unhealthy eating habits and the unhealthy relationship we have with food. Saying that eating less is easier said than done is why I am proposing a paradigm shift on how introducing faith into our lives can change important aspects of our lives.

CHAPTER 12

"You Son of a Black Slave Woman"

On one occasion after a battle, Abu Dhar, who was an emotional and tribal Arab, was at a gathering that included Belal, an Ethiopian slave and a companion to the Prophet Muhammed. The group was discussing what to do with the spoils of a battle. After each person gave their opinion, Abu Dhar had a diverging opinion. When it came to Belal, he gave his opinion of what should be done with the spoils. His opinion was also different from Abu Dhar's. This angered Abu Dhar and in an unadulterated outburst, he said, "And you too, Belal, you son of a black slave woman." This racial epithet hurt Belal very much and he withdrew from the gathering.

In our times, we would call Belal a wimp or a snitch, but being a student of the Prophet, he knew what he was doing. He went to the Prophet Muhammad to complain. Upon hearing this, the Prophet went out into the public market. When he saw Abu Dhar, he said, "Did you call Belal, so and so." Abu Dhar, seeing the displeasure of the Prophet's face, admitted his outburst. The Prophet said "Abu Dhar, you are a man who still has traces of Jahiliya in you." Ignorance here doesn't just mean lack of knowledge or insensitivity; it also means something rabidly anti-Islamic. Jahiliya was the time before Islam when the Arabs not only worshipped other gods but had no sense of right and wrong, and it caused them to do things that were anti-Islamic in behavior. They fought along tribal lines over the most trivial of matters, they mistreated their women and, in some cases, buried their infant daughters alive.

This response of the Prophet was very injurious to Abu Dhar. We may have expected Abu Dhar to be angry with Belal or resentful, maybe to confront him. Abu Dhar immediately sought out Belal in the open market and said, "By God, I have wronged you." He placed his head on the ground and said, "I will not move my neck until you place your foot over it, so everyone can see that Abu Dhar has been belittled and Belal has been raised." According to the tradition, Belal gets on his knees, kisses Abu Dhar's forehead, and says, "Abu Dhar, No, I forgive you."

It is ironic that expressions of racial superiority, associated with the past, flourish in a modern, free, and open society such as America. The idea that some human beings are superior to other human beings solely on the basis of skin color is a troubling one. While not restricted to white nationalism, the kind of racism associated with white European exploitation and settlement of inhabited land, supplantation of the indigenous inhabitants, the introduction of slavery, and a system of segregation along racial lines is a unique historical manifestation of racism in America.

In addition to the notion of white superiority, other factors have made American racism stand out over other forms of racism. For example, America's historical identification with Christianity, a religion associated with love, sacrifice, and charity, highlights a glaring contradiction between Christian teachings of racial harmony and racism. Slavery, while prevalent throughout the world before its abolishment, was more grievous in America to the extent that it specifically targeted black Africans over other races. Despite emancipation, equal rights were denied to black Americans for over a century later. Moreover, American racism has continued to exist as America peddles its prodemocratic credentials to a world population yearning for genuine freedom from oppression, war, and poverty.

There is an old saying "I hear your words and I am smitten with love. I see your actions and I am appalled."

Beyond the hypocrisy abroad is an underlying domestic issue some term "the browning of America." As the minority population increases, especially Hispanic, white Americans are fearful of losing their power base, culture influence, and financial capital. Decreasing numbers of any previously dominant group is scary. It was scary for the indigenous native populations when their numbers dramatically dwindled two centuries ago, and it's scary today for white Americans.

So, while other groups throughout the world exhibit racism and discrimination, none of them claim racial superiority, confess Christianity, promote democracy, and have military deployments in over 70 percent of the world's countries (McCarthy) (Gibbons-Neff).

Racism in America is endemic. The statistics bear this out (Gal). The results of racism are also clear. People of color, especially black people, are more likely to be convicted and incarcerated for the same offenses, placed in lower paying jobs despite similar education levels, and physically abused or killed by law enforcement (DoSomething.org). Racial discrimination affects its victims physically, psychologically, economically, and politically.

Racism comes in the form of many different expressions. The one that is more insidious is the belief that different races possess distinct characteristics, abilities, or qualities, especially so as to distinguish them as inferior or superior to one another. Oftentimes, this belief leads to prejudice, discrimination, or antagonism directed against a person or people on the basis of their membership in a particular racial or ethnic group, typically one that is a minority or marginalized (Oxford Languages).

Muslims are not free of racism. They have their own manifestations that lead to discrimination and prejudice against others. In Islam, though, as we see from the story of Abu Dharr and Belal, the Prophet Muhammad appropriately dealt with instances of racism. The most definitive response to racism appears in the Qur'anic verse "O mankind, verily, We created you from male and female, and We made you into nations and tribes to get to know one another. The best of you in the sight of God are the most mindful (of Him). God is Knowing and Aware." *Qur'an* 49:13 From personal experience and studies, we know that getting to know others (the absence of ignorance) tends to alleviate fear, hatred, discrimination, and racism.

In terms of practice, Muslim empires ruled over a diverse group of ethnicities and races. The Ottoman Empire, which lasted over six hundred years, incorporated dozens of ethnicities and was the most religiously diverse empire in Europe and Asia (Kieser).

Like Christians, Muslims are a very diverse group of people spanning the globe and accounting for nearly one-fourth of its population. In America, mosques are ethnically diverse, and Muslims are the most likely to enter into interracial marriages (Bagby) (Chouhoud).

Muslims in America are very sensitive to racism and discrimination. According to Pew, "Two-thirds of Muslims in the United States (67 percent) say the country needs to continue making changes to give blacks equal rights with whites, a higher percentage than the share of Americans in general who say this (57 percent)" (Diamant).

Islam has its own claim to superior behavior. It's not predicated on race. It is the concept that the best of human beings are the ones who are most conscious of God.

Racism is a disease, and it's bad, but you can't eradicate it with legislation or violence. It can only be stemmed with education, engagement, and sincerity in working for all human beings.

One of the greatest personalities in modern times is reflected in the character and development of Malcolm X. He went from being an Afro-Nationalist to a mainstream Muslim.

He was a man among males, a hero among men, and a role model among heroes. If anyone could've brought the white supremacists to the table, it would've been him because he was the epitome of the good they claim to champion. After breaking off with the Nation of Islam, he went on the Pilgrimage (Hajj) to Mecca in 1964. That experience changed his life and his views. In accepting mainstream Islam, he no longer preached that the white man was the devil. He said that on the Hajj he saw the blackest of black and the whitest of white in harmony, eating, drinking, and worshipping together.

He is not alone in his experience. When I performed Hajj for the first time in 2001, I was truly amazed being among two million people at one time, in one place coming for the same reason—to worship God. The men are required to wear two pieces of white cloth without seams, hems, or buttons. For ease of movement, women are allowed to wear any comfortable clothing. With this simplicity, it was almost impossible to differentiate between others' economic, social, or political status.

Islam has taught me to respect other religions and other people and their ways of life. Living in America for half a century has allowed me to learn about this country and those who built and led it. "Manifest Destiny" is romanticized by some into a narrative of Christians fleeing persecution, building a democracy, and conquering the land for civilization from one end of the continent to the other. We know this entailed ethnic cleansing, racism, and slavery.

However, this does not detract from the millions of white Americans who tilled the soil, explored the continent, settled on farms and in cities to work hard, and fought and died for what they had achieved for themselves and their families. A great nation was born. However, nothing can excuse racism or oppression. If I was a white nationalist trying to set things straight, I would go out of my way not to be self-hating but to show justice for others. People aspire to many lofty ideals about freedom, rights, happiness, and wealth, but what everyone really wants is to be dignified and treated justly by those in power. Islam calls on everyone to practice showing each other dignity and fairness.

Conclusion

Death is a part of life, and we will all taste death. We may not know when, where or how we will die, however, we have some control over the state or disposition we are in when the time comes. Are we happy, sad, regretful, fulfilled, afraid or welcoming?

Faith is also a part of life.

One may choose to approach faith with a Pascalian wager model; believe, what do you have to lose?

Faith in God is above and beyond our reasoned arguments, for or against. Faith in Islam while an individual choice calls on the human being to use reason comprehensively, not limiting it to empirical knowledge of what we know.

In offering some insight into Islam I have introduced the reader to certain Islamic concepts about faith, justice, and human nature. At a minimum one should take what good may be extracted from Muslim teachings and use it in the best way to improve one's life, and the society we all share.

The challenge of Islam for America is for America to live up to the best standards and morality it can. It's irrelevant if Muslims fall short in practicing their faith, I have presented Islam according to its core mainstream understanding. Peoples of the Muslim world in order to change their state of affairs should stop blaming America and the West for their current internal situation, and here in America we should accept responsibility and reform our nation of the racism, greed and immorality fueling economic disparity, the war on civil liberties and violence at home and abroad.

If we demand of Muslims to reform and look inwards, we need to do the same.

It's psychologically challenging to see the human advancement we have achieved and not feel immense pride and satisfaction, however, such arrogance has to be tempered by humility. Every advancement we have achieved can be destroyed in the blink of an eye, by natural causes or through our own actions. As we are motivated to zealously promote, advance, and establish individual rights and freedoms we should show the same enthusiasm in imposing self-restraint and accountability. Let us practice our own self-imposed checks and balances on our intentions and actions.

Hold yourself accountable before you are held to account.

Islam, with its built-in mechanisms for accountability, gives one the tools necessary to live a fulfilling, meaningful and successful life. Whether by Islam or some other means you must want a fulfilling life, or at least enough endurance to avoid despair.

Western heritage, over the millenniums offers a path to this goal, but, is an incomplete guide to a successful personal and communal life.

Another reason to temper our over-confidence is to remember what goes around comes around. One day is for you, one day is against you. The life of a civilization is no different.

The once mighty Roman empire was identified with the motto "Unconquered Rome." Before it, Alexander the Great's motto was "There is nothing impossible to him who will try."

Not only did the Muslim armies reconquer all of Rome's eastern provinces, and north Africa, Arabs raided Rome itself. Today nearly all the territory included in Alexander the Great's vast empire has been subsumed and inherited by the Muslim world. Even Greece was occupied by the Muslim Ottoman empire for nearly four hundred years, until just a couple of centuries ago.

After the setback of the Middle Ages, the European renaissance picked up the western flag of progress. The motto of the renaissance was "back to the source" as if to say back to basics, back to the fundamentals—a rebirth. The Muslim preservation, translation and original contributions to Greek philosophy and scientific advancement enabled the renaissance to flourish (Faruqi). In turn, the industrial revolution and European imperialism owe their inspiration to the renaissance that gravitated from being God centered to man centered (Encyclopedia.com).

From the end of the 20th century America has picked up the banner of western civilization. From Greek democracy to Christianity to neo-liberalism what is the motto of the U.S?

"In God we Trust"

Obviously, many will say its outdated.

We should either change the motto or infuse it in a secular context that allows for sincerity, morality, and the dignity of the human being; the religious one as well. Otherwise, we will be supplanted by others who work harder for the truth and achieve greater justice.

The greatest problems threatening the disintegration of American society include glaring political division, racism, violence, acute economic disparity, alcohol abuse and drug addiction, gender confusion and sexual promiscuity. Bear in mind no one can stop you from taking drugs or engaging in all kinds of "legal" sexual relationships with other adults by consent, experimenting with your gender or greedily chasing after money. The question is why do you want to do such things?

To solve such problems and attain a healthy society, Islam offers prescriptive principles and guidelines to consider.

Any undertaking, including societal change, begins with the individual. And everyone has an intention, so intentions should be good intentions based on a solid morale code. Each one of us should humble ourselves to something greater than ourselves.

I would say God.

You may not believe in God. You know you did not create yourself, so, begin by humbling yourself to the possibilities.

Humbleness makes one a calmer person inwardly and towards others.

Once humbled it becomes easier to empathize with others and situations. We become discerning of news that we hear from the mainstream media, social media, and the vast majority of agenda-ridden content. Do not accept information without vetting it for accuracy and evaluate it through the lens of a realistic and healthy world view. Failure to do this leads to misunderstanding, hostile feelings, and bad decisions. These bad decisions end up harming people in society.

Our principles of what's right and wrong must be strong enough that we are willing to fight as a last resort. Two groups may fight each other. It's our job to make peace between them. However, if one group becomes recalcitrant and attacks the other group, then we must fight the transgressing party until it ceases its hostility. When it realizes its culpability then make peace between the groups in all fairness and justice.

Societies will always have disputing parties but it must also have arbitrators. Truth and justice require champions to uphold them.

If the republican and democratic parties come to blows among each other over the many issues dividing the nation, who can save the day except strong-willed moral leaders?

We are all human beings deserving of fairness from those who have leadership over us.

Empathy can help to prevent us from reaching a point of violence. A person who possesses empathy and a strong sense of justice is the qualified type of leader who if forced to resort to violence does so with a consensus that he or she was justified.

We need such leaders in America who can transcend racial and cultural loyalties.

Human beings tend to organize themselves along racial, ethnic and linguistic lines. As a tendency this is natural. If someone looks similar to you, speaks like you do and shares the same traditions and culture that you do, you are more likely to approach, bond with and understand such person than someone who is further away from you in these characteristics.

However, the line is drawn when we realize that this familiarity can be a weakness and problematic. If such "tribal" identification causes you to feel superior to others, arrogant and an inability to judge objectively then this is a problem.

Superiority should require that a group works for the rest of humanity to increase the education, well-being, and dignity of other human beings. Why didn't white America do more to educate, nurture and share with the newly emancipated black population, the backbone of the nation's progress, the advantages and prosperity that only some of us enjoy today? What's responsible, Christianity, secularism or perhaps racism?

Many in America saw the native population and African Americans as inferior. This allowed groups to deride and ridicule other groups. Such behavior today is hidden behind freedom of speech.

While we pride ourselves in the West about the sanctity of freedom of speech, we don't know how to practice it. Just because I can make fun of others or insult peoples' sensibilities, why should I? The irony, with tragic circumstances, would be if the group being ridiculed turns out to be better than the group doing the ridiculing.

This arrogant sense of superiority and sarcasm further erodes societal bonds.

One of the most overlooked vices plaguing society is spying whether as individuals or most important as groups or governments. Spying becomes a tool by which one group controls another group. If our government finds it necessary to surveille its population that means its afraid of losing its power and vested interests—interests that aren't in the interest of the majority. The best way to avoid this vice is to always do what's in the interest of the people.

And the people have to strive to align their interests with the timeless moralities of truth, justice, freedom and peace.

Americans and Muslims want the same things.

If Islam—most associated with submission to and worship of the one God—were to have a motto for human beings it would be this one simple chapter (sura) of the Qur'an—because nothing is as powerful as an idea whose time has come.

"(I swear) by time. The human being is in utter loss. Except those who believe, do good, and counsel each other unto truth and counsel each other to be constant in patience."

QUR'AN CHAPTER 103

Acknowledgments

He who does not thank people does not thank God. I am grateful to the many supportive individuals around me including my immediate family, extended family, and all those who are just like family. They know who they are and the good intentions, encouragement, and feedback they have provided for this humble work. And special thanks to Ambata Kazi Nance, who reviewed, edited, and provided valuable feedback every step of the way.

Appendix

INTRODUCTION

Ali, Hassan. "Muslim Roots of America." Accessed on Oct. 19, 2021. https://digitalcommons.murraystate.edu/cgi/viewcontent.cgi?article=1150&context=bis437

Amini, Miriam. "At Stake in US Military Efforts to Stabilize Afghanistan: At Least $3 Trillion in Natural Resources." Accessed Oct. 19, 2021. https://www.cnbc.com/2017/08/18/trumps-afghanistan-strategy-may-unlock-3-trillion-in-natural-resources.html

Answering Christianity. "Honor Killings in the Bible." Accessed Oct. 19, 2021. https://answeringchristian.wordpress.com/2012/01/11/honor-killing-was-inspired-from-bible/

Cartwright, Mark. "The Capture of Jerusalem, 1099 CE." Accessed Oct. 19, 2021. https://www.ancient.eu/article/1254/the-capture-of-jerusalem-1099-ce/

Copoglu, Sumeyye. "10 Things You Use Every Day That Are Invented by Muslims." Accessed Oct. 19, 2021. https://mvslim.com/10-things-you-use-every-day-that-are-invented-by-muslims/

Dajani-Shakeel, Hadia. "Some Medieval Accounts of Salah al-Din's Recovery of Jerusalem (Al-Quds)." Accessed on Oct. 19, 2021. https://sourcebooks.fordham.edu/med/salahdin.asp

DMDC. Stats Report. Accessed Oct. 19, 2021. https://www.dmdc.osd.mil/appj/dwp/stats_reports.jsp

Encyclopaedia Britannica Online. "The Crusader States to 1187." Accessed Oct. 19, 2021. https://www.britannica.com/event/Crusades/The-Crusader-states-to-1187

Everts, Sarah. "Europe's Hypocritical History of Cannibalism." Accessed Oct. 19, 2021. https://www.smithsonianmag.com/history/europes-hypocritical-history-of-cannibalism-42642371/

Fordham University. "Medieval Sourcebook: The Siege and Capture of Jerusalem: Collected Accounts." Accessed Oct. 19, 2021. https://sourcebooks.fordham.edu/source/cde-jlem.asp

Georgetown University. "The Bridge Initiative: Two Decades of Americans' Views on Islam & Muslims." Accessed Oct. 19, 2021. https://bridge.georgetown.edu/wp-content/uploads/2018/11/The-Super-Survey.pdf

Global Policy Forum. "US Military and Clandestine Operations in Foreign Countries—1798–Present." Accessed Oct. 19,

2021. https://www.globalpolicy.org/us-westward-expansion/26024-us-interventions.html

Grossman, Zoltan. "From Wounded Knee to Syria: US Military Interventions Since 1890." Accessed Oct. 19, 2021. https://sites.evergreen.edu/zoltan/interventions/

Gross, Terry. NPR Fresh Air Podcast. Interview with Stephen Kinzer, "The History of US Intervention and the 'Birth of the American Empire.'" Jan. 24, 2017. Podcast. https://www.npr.org/2017/01/24/511387528/the-history-of-u-s-intervention-and-the-birth-of-the-american-empire

Hugo, Victor. *Histoire d'un Crime* (The History of a Crime). Translated by T.H. Joyce and Arthur Locker. [written 1852, published 1877]. https://www.thesciencefaith.com/honor-killing-in-the-bible/

Humanities and Social Sciences Online. "African Muslim Slaves in America." Accessed Oct. 19, 2021. https://networks.h-net.org/node/28765/pages/31928/african-muslim-slaves-america

Ibrahim, Arwa. "All You Need to Know about the OIC." Accessed Oct. 19, 2021. https://www.aljazeera.com/news/2019/5/31/all-you-need-to-know-about-the-oic#:~:text=It%20was%20established%20by%2024,population%20reaching%20over%201.8%20billion

Jefferies, Stuart. "The Muslims Who Shaped America—From Brain Surgeons to Rappers." Accessed Oct. 10, 2021. https://www.theguardian.com/world/2015/dec/08/donald-trump-famous-muslims-us-history

Kelly, Victoria. "Fun Facts about Countries with Biggest US Military Bases." Accessed Oct. 19, 2021. https://www.sandboxx.us/blog/fun-facts-about-countries-with-biggest-us-military-bases/

Khan, Syed. "Saladin's Conquest of Jerusalem (1187 CE)." Accessed Oct. 19, 2021. https://www.ancient.eu/article/1553/saladins-conquest-of-jerusalem-1187-ce/

Nations Online. Countries and Regions of the World from A to Z. Accessed Oct. 19, 2021. https://www.nationsonline.org/oneworld/countries_of_the_world.htm#:~:text=How%20many%20countries%20are%20there,several%20disputed%20territories%2C%20like%20Kosovo

PRB. World Population Data Sheet 2020. Accessed Oct. 19, 2021. https://www.prb.org/2020-world-population-data-sheet/#:~:text=The%20world%20population%20is%20projected,as%20in%20the%20United%20States

Quick, Abdullah. "The African, and Muslim, Discovery of America—Before Columbus." Accessed Oct. 19, 2021. https://historyofislam.com/the-african-and-muslim-discovery-of-america-before-columbus/

Rosenberg, Yair. "The Complicated History of Thomas Jefferson's Koran." Accessed Oct. 19, 2021. https://www.washingtonpost.com/outlook/2019/01/02/complicated-history-thomas-jeffersons-koran/

Rubenstein, Jay. "Cannibals and Crusaders." Accessed Oct. 19, 2021. http://courses.washington.edu/holywar/Links_files/Cannibals%20and%20Crusaders.pdf

Savell, Stephanie and 5W Infographics. "This Map Shows Where in the World the US Military Is Combatting Terrorism." Accessed Oct. 19, 2021. https://www.smithsonianmag.com/history/map-shows-places-world-where-us-military-operates-180970997/

Schleifer, Theodore. "Donald Trump: 'I think Islam Hates Us.'" Accessed Oct. 19, 2021. https://www.cnn.com/2016/03/09/politics/donald-trump-islam-hates-us/index.html

West, Julia. "Threat of Muslim-American Terrorism Remains Low." Accessed Oct. 19, 2021. https://www.hsdl.org/c/threat-of-muslim-american-terrorism-remains-low/

Williams, Jennifer. "A Brief History of Islam in America." Accessed Oct. 19, 2021. https://www.vox.com/2015/12/22/10645956/islam-in-america

HOW TO READ THIS BOOK

Pew Research Center. "The Future of World Religions: Population Growth Projections, 2010–2050." Accessed Oct. 19, 2021. https://www.pewforum.org/2015/04/02/religious-projections-2010-2050/

CHAPTER 2

Barford, Vanessa. "**Iran's 'diagnosed transsexuals.'**" Feb. 25, 2008. http://news.bbc.co.uk/2/hi/7259057.stm

Burchell, Victoria. "Polygamy Left Its Mark on Human Genome." Sept. 29, 2014. https://www.bionews.org.uk/page_94760

Castleman, Michael. "Why Men Are Hot for Sex but Women Warm to It." Accessed Oct. 10, 2020. https://www.aarp.org/home-family/sex-intimacy/info-2014/sexual-desire-and-gender-castleman.html

Foreign Affairs Manual. "9 FAM 302.12." Sept. 10, 2021. https://fam.state.gov/fam/09FAM/09FAM030212.html

Guillen, Lina. "Federal Marriage Benefits Available to Same-Sex Couples." Accessed Oct. 20, 2020. https://www.nolo.com/legal-encyclopedia/same-sex-couples-federal-marriage-benefits-30326.html

Hagan, Ekua. "Why Are There Virtually No Polyandrous Societies?" Jun. 5, 2008. https://www.psychologytoday.com/us/blog/the-scientific-fundamentalist/200806/why-are-there-virtually-no-polyandrous-societies#:~:text=A%20comprehensive%20survey%20of%20traditional,of%20brothers%20share%20a%20wife

Hammer, Michael, Fernando L. Mendez, Murray P. Cox, August E. Woerner, and Jeffrey D. Wall. "Sex-Biased Evolutionary Forces Shape Genomic Patterns of Human Diversity."

Sept. 26, 2008. https://journals.plos.org/plosgenetics/article?id=10.1371/journal.pgen.1000202

Holder, Kathleen. "Often decried, polygyny may sometimes have advantages." Oct. 29, 2015. https://www.sciencedaily.com/releases/2015/10/151029102240.htm#:~:text=When%20comparing%20households%20within%20individual,more%20land%20than%20monogamous%20households

Imani, Faizah. "How Cheating Affects the Workplace." Accessed Oct. 20, 2020. https://work.chron.com/cheating-affects-workplace-7456.html

Labuda, Damian, Jean-FrançoisLefebvre, PhilippeNadeau, and Marie-HélèneRoy-Gagnon. "Female-to-Male Breeding Ratio in Modern Humans—an Analysis Based on Historical Recombinations." Jan. 29, 2010. https://www.sciencedirect.com/science/article/pii/S0002929710000339

Lawson, David, Susan James, Esther Ngadaya, Bernard Ngowi, Sayoki G. M. Mfinanga, and Monique Borgerhoff Mulder. "No evidence that polygynous marriage is a harmful cultural practice in northern Tanzania." Nov. 10, 2015. https://www.pnas.org/content/112/45/13827

Newport, Frank. "Understanding the Increase in Moral Acceptability of Polygamy." Jun. 26, 2020. https://news.gallup.com/opinion/polling-matters/313112/understanding-increase-moral-acceptability-polygamy.aspx

Schacht, Ryan and Karen L. Kramer. "Are We Monogamous? A Review of the Evolution of Pair-Bonding in Humans and

Its Contemporary Variation Cross-Culturally." Jul. 17, 2019. https://www.frontiersin.org/articles/10.3389/fevo.2019.00230/full

Sine, Richard. "Sex Drive: How Do Men and Women Compare?" Aug. 22, 2013. https://www.webmd.com/sex/features/sex-drive-how-do-men-women-compare#1

US Citizenship and Immigration Services. "Same-Sex Marriages." Jul. 1, 2013. https://www.uscis.gov/family/same-sex-marriages#:~:text=Yes.,the%20United%20States%20for%20marriage

van Anders. Sari M. "Testosterone and sexual desire in healthy women and men." May 3, 2012. https://pubmed.ncbi.nlm.nih.gov/22552705/

Vile, John R. "Morrill Anti-bigamy Act of 1862 (1862)." Accessed Oct. 20, 2020. https://www.mtsu.edu/first-amendment/article/1040/morrill-anti-bigamy-act-of-1862

CHAPTER 3
West, J. and D. I. Templer. "Child Molestation, Rape, and Ethnicity." Accessed on Oct. 19, 2021. https://pubmed.ncbi.nlm.nih.gov/7892399/

CHAPTER 4
Erlanger, Steven. "Palestinian Held in US May Halt Fight on Extradition." Accessed Oct. 19, 2021. https://www.nytimes.

com/1997/01/29/world/palestinian-held-in-us-may-halt-fight-on-extradition.html

Gellman, Barton. "Israel No Longer Wants US To Extradite Hamas Leader." *The Washington Post*, April 1997. Accessed Oct. 19, 2021. http://tech.mit.edu/V117/N16/israel.16w.html

Justia Law. "Matter of Extradition of Marzook, 924 F. Supp. 565 (S.D.N.Y. 1996)." Accessed on Oct. 19, 2021. https://law.justia.com/cases/federal/district-courts/FSupp/924/565/1471825/

CHAPTER 5

Buchinger Wilhelmi Clinic I The Fasting Experts. "Scientific Review: 100 Years of Clinical Fasting Experience and Latest Research (2020)." Jul 27, 2020. https://www.youtube.com/watch?v=6EQmzNgX90c

Bunn, Mark. Ancient Wisdom from Modern Health Podcast. "Gut Health & Microbiome: Ayurveda & Modern Science with Prof Keith Wallace." Jun. 16, 2021. Podcast. https://markbunn.com.au/blog/gut-health-microbiome-ayurveda-and-modern-science-with-professor-keith-wallace

Coca-Cola Nederland. "Coca-Cola Sunset." May 17, 2018. https://www.youtube.com/watch?v=oXDI1l_zjkA

Ho, K, et al. "Fasting Enhances Growth Hormone Secretion and Amplifies the Complex Rhythms of Growth Hormone Secretion in Man." Accessed Oct. 19, 2021. https://www.ncbi.nlm.nih.gov/pmc/articles/PMC329619/

Lanyan, Charley. "The Brain-Gut Connection: How TCM Has Known for Centuries What Western Medicine Is Now Discovering." Accessed Oct. 19, 2021. https://www.scmp.com/lifestyle/health-wellness/article/3022925/brain-gut-connection-how-tcm-has-known-centuries-what

Pietrocola, Federico, et. al. "Metabolic Effects of Fasting on Human and Mouse Blood in Vivo." Accessed Oct. 19, 2021. https://www.tandfonline.com/doi/full/10.1080/15548627.2016.1271513

Saeed, Madiha. "The PropheticRx Guide to Healing the Prophetic (S) Way!" Accessed Oct. 19, 2021. https://holisticmommd.com/propheticrx-guide-healing-prophetic-s-way/

University of California Television (UCTV). "Sugar: The Bitter Truth." Jul 30, 2009. https://www.youtube.com/watch?v=dBnniua6-oM

US Department of Agriculture: Economic Research Service. "Food Loss." Accessed Oct. 19, 2021. https://www.ers.usda.gov/data-products/food-availability-per-capita-data-system/food-loss/

Vendelbo, Mikkel, et. al. "Fasting Increases Human Skeletal Muscle Net Phenylalanine Release and This Is Associated with Decreased mTOR Signaling." Accessed Oct. 19, 2021. https://journals.plos.org/plosone/article?id=10.1371/journal.pone.0102031

CHAPTER 6

AFP and TOI Staff. "Mashaal Says Hamas Will Not Speak to Israel Directly." Sep. 12, 2014. https://www.timesofisrael.com/mashaal-says-hamas-will-not-speak-to-israel-directly/

Agha, Zena. "Israel's Problematic Role in Perpetuating Water Insecurity for Palestine." Jun. 28, 2019. https://www.atlanticcouncil.org/blogs/menasource/israel-s-problematic-role-in-perpetuating-water-insecurity-for-palestine/

Ahmad, Irfan. "How the West De-Democratised the Middle East." Mar. 30, 2012. https://www.aljazeera.com/opinions/2012/3/30/how-the-west-de-democratised-the-middle-east

Aked, Hilary. "The Undeniable Overlap: Right-Wing Zionism and Islamophobia." Sept. 29, 2015. https://www.opendemocracy.net/en/undeniable-overlap-right-wing-zionism-and-islamophobia/

al-Zahar, Mahmoud. "No Peace Without Hamas." *Washington Post*. Apr. 17, 2008. https://www.washingtonpost.com/wp-dyn/content/article/2008/04/16/AR2008041602899.html

Andrews, Edward. "Christian Missions and Colonial Empires Reconsidered: A Black Evangelist in West Africa, 1766–1816." *Journal of Church and State*, Volume 51, Issue 4, Autumn 2009, Pages 663–691. https://academic.oup.com/jcs/article-abstract/51/4/663/793842?redirectedFrom=fulltext

Arlosoroff, Meirav. "Israel to Regulate So-called 'Grey Market' Loan Sharks." Mar. 6, 2017. https://www.haaretz.com/israel-news/business/israel-to-regulate-so-called-grey-market-loan-sharks-1.5445234

Auerbach, Shakked. "Israeli Porn Is Booming, and the Industry Insists It's about More Than Just Sex." Accessed Oct. 19,2021. https://www.haaretz.com/life/.premium.MAGAZINE-israeli-porn-is-booming-and-the-industry-insists-it-s-about-more-than-just-sex-1.5472336

Bazian, Hatem. "The Islamophobia Industry and the Demonization of Palestine: Implications for American Studies." *Johns Hopkins University Press*, Volume 67, Number 4, December 2015. https://muse.jhu.edu/article/605051

Beauchamp, Zack. "Why the US Has the Most Pro-Israel Foreign Policy in the World." Accessed Oct. 19, 2021. https://www.vox.com/2014/7/24/5929705/us-israel-friends

Bennis, Phyllis. "Opinion: I'm Jewish. I Fight Anti-Semitism and I Support Palestinian Rights." *LA Times*, Dec. s6, 2019. https://www.latimes.com/opinion/story/2019-12-26/anti-semitism-donald-trump-jews-executive-order

Bethancourt, Phillip. "Christ the Warrior King: A Biblical, Historical, and Theological Analysis of the Divine Warrior Theme in Christology." Sept. 2010. https://sbts-wordpress-uploads.s3.amazonaws.com/sbts/uploads/sites/26/2012/07/bethancourt-christ-the-warrior-king-prospectus.pdf

Brenneman, Jonathan. "Anti-Semitic Zionists." March 10, 2019. https://www.dandc.eu/en/article/how-evangelicals-have-usurped-jewish-americans-support-israel

Bruton, F. "Holy Land Christians Feel Abandoned by US Evangelicals." May 5, 2018. https://www.nbcnews.com/news/world/holy-land-christians-feel-abandoned-u-s-evangelicals-n867371

Bump, Phillip. "Half of Evangelicals Support Israel Because They Believe It Is Important for Fulfilling End-Times Prophecy." Accessed Oct. 19, 2019. https://www.washingtonpost.com/news/politics/wp/2018/05/14/half-of-evangelicals-support-israel-because-they-believe-it-is-important-for-fulfilling-end-times-prophecy/

Carter, Jimmy. "Israel, Palestine, Peace and Apartheid." Dec. 11, 2006. Accessed Oct. 19, 2021. https://www.theguardian.com/commentisfree/2006/dec/12/israel.politicsphilosophyandsociety

Christianity Today. "Crisis Evangelism in Latin America." Nov. 23, 1962. https://www.christianitytoday.com/ct/1962/november-23/crisis-evangelism-in-latin-america.html

Christians United for Israel. "Home Page." Accessed Oct. 19, 2021. https://cufi.org/

Cole, David. "The Roberts Court vs. Free Speech." *The New York Review.* Aug. 19, 2010. https://www.nybooks.com/articles/2010/08/19/roberts-court-vs-free-speech/

Cook, Jonathan. "How Evangelical Christians Risk Setting the Middle East on Fire." July 8, 2019. https://www.middleeasteye.net/opinion/how-evangelical-christians-risk-setting-middle-east-fire

Corradin, Camilla. "Israel: Water as a Tool to Dominate Palestinians." Jun. 23, 2016. https://www.aljazeera.com/news/2016/6/23/israel-water-as-a-tool-to-dominate-palestinians

Cortellessa, Eric. "New Poll: Americans' Support for Israel Falls to Lowest Point in a Decade." Mar. 6. 2019. https://www.timesofisrael.com/new-poll-americans-support-for-israel-declines-to-lowest-point-in-a-decade/

Daily History. "When Did Constantine the Great Really Become a Christian?" Accessed Oct. 19, 2021. https://dailyhistory.org/When_did_Constantine_the_Great_really_become_a_Christian%3F

Debusmann, Bernd. "Hamas Scores Publicity Coup in US." June 22, 2007. https://www.reuters.com/article/us-usa-hamas/hamas-scores-publicity-coup-in-u-s-idUSN2248322920070622

Editorial. "Mr. Zahar and Mr. Carter." *Washington Post*. April 17, 2008. https://www.washingtonpost.com/wp-dyn/content/article/2008/04/16/AR2008041603097.html

Grinker, Roy, Stephen Lubkemann, and Christopher Steiner. *Perspective of Africa: A Reader in Culture, History, and Representation*. Blackwell Publishing Ltd., 1997. https://books.google.com/books?id=myLOFYZ4dQoC&pg=PA31#v=onepage&q&f=false

Haaretz. "Israel among the Least Religious Countries in the World." Apr. 14, 2015. https://www.haaretz.com/israel-china-among-least-religious-nations-1.5350737

Harb, Ali. "Meet the Candidates Challenging Pro-Israel Democrats in US Congress." *Middle East Eye*, May 26, 2020. Accessed Oct. 19, 2021. https://www.middleeasteye.net/news/meet-challengers-taking-pro-israel-democrats-us-congress

Hazzan, David. "Christianity and Korea." April 7, 2016. https://thediplomat.com/2016/04/christianity-and-korea/

Heather, Peter. "Divine Victory: The Role of Christianity in Roman Military Conquests." June 12, 2018. https://blog.oup.com/2018/06/divine-victory-christianity-rome/

Heller, Jeffrey. "Jews, Arabs Nearing Population Parity in Holy Land: Israeli Officials." Mar. 26, 2018. https://www.reuters.com/article/us-israel-palestinians-population/jews-arabs-nearing-population-parity-in-holy-land-israeli-officials-idUSKBN1H222T

Holder v. Humanitarian Law Project, 561 US 1 (2010). https://www.oyez.org/cases/2009/08-1498

ICT Staff. "Pope Francis Apologizes to Indigenous Peoples for 'Grave Sins' of Colonialism." Jul. 10, 2015. https://indiancountrytoday.com/archive/pope-francis-apologizes-to-indigenous-peoples-for-grave-sins-of-colonialism-tl-GAXDXgwkCkvmn10DjT3Q

Inbari, Motti. "Why Do Evangelicals Support Israel?" Cambridge University Press, Jan. 14, 2020. https://www.cambridge.org/core/journals/politics-and-religion/article/abs/why-do-evangelicals-support-israel/F8AB8C41F0B019F-D8413A30EF218EBE4

Islamophobia Research & Documentation Project. "Zionism Funds Islamophobia Postcars." Accessed Oct. 19, 2021. https://irdproject.com/wp-content/uploads/2019/09/Zionism-Funds-Islamophobia-Postcard-318286-v1.pdf

Jewish & Non-Jewish Population of Israel/Palestine (1517–Present). Jewish Virtual Library. Accessed on Oct. 19, 2021. https://www.jewishvirtuallibrary.org/jewish-and-non-jewish-population-of-israel-palestine-1517-present

Jewish Voice for Peace. "Resources." Accessed Oct. 19, 2021. https://jewishvoiceforpeace.org/network-against-islamophobia/

Judis, John. "Clueless in Gaza." Feb. 19, 2013. https://newrepublic.com/article/112456/george-w-bushs-secret-war-against-hamas

Kessler, Ed. "Jesus the Jew." Accessed Oct. 19, 2021. http://www.bbc.co.uk/thepassion/articles/jesus_the_jew.shtml

Kotch, Alex. "Ilhan Omar Is Right about the Influence of the Israel Lobby." Feb. 13, 2019. https://www.theguardian.com/commentisfree/2019/feb/13/ilhan-omar-is-right-about-the-influence-of-the-israel-lobby

Lerner, Michael. "Jews against Zionism—an Intro to Their Perspective." Mar. 7, 2014. https://www.tikkun.org/jews-against-zionism-an-intro-to-their-perspective

Martin, Michel. *All Things Considered.* "The Influence of American Jewish Attitudes on Israeli Politics." April 13, 2019. Podcast. https://www.npr.org/2019/04/13/713097748/the-influence-of-american-jewish-attitudes-on-israeli-politics

Marzook, Mousa. "Hamas Speak." *LA Times.* Jan. 6, 2009. https://www.latimes.com/opinion/la-oe-marzook6-2009jan06-story.html

Marzook, Mousa. "Hamas Stand." *LA Times.* Jul. 10, 2007. https://www.latimes.com/la-oe-marzook10jul10-story.html

Marzook, Mousa. "What Hamas Is Seeking." *Washington Post.* Jan. 31, 2006. https://www.washingtonpost.com/wp-dyn/content/article/2006/01/30/AR2006013001209.html

Movsesian, Mark. "Fiqh and Canons: Reflections on Islamic and Christian Jurisprudence." 2010. Accessed Oct. 19, 2021. https://scholarship.law.stjohns.edu/faculty_publications/97/

National Archives. "The Bill of Rights: A Transcription." Accessed Oct. 19, 2021. https://www.archives.gov/founding-docs/bill-of-rights-transcript

Norton, Ben. "Support for Palestinians Growing among Young, Progressive Americans, Pew Report Finds." Salon.com, May 6, 2016. https://www.salon.com/2016/05/06/support_for_palestinians_growing_among_young_progressive_americans_pew_report_finds/

Obidallah, Mohammed. "Water and the Palestinian-Israeli Conflict." *Columbia*. Accessed Oct. 19, 2021. http://www.columbia.edu/~tmd2118/situstudio/m.obidallah_water_and_conflict.pdf

Pappe, Ilan. *The Ethnic Cleansing of Palestine*. Oneworld Publication, 2007. https://www.amazon.com/Ethnic-Cleansing-Palestine-Ilan-Pappe/dp/1851685553

Pew Research Center. "In US, Decline of Christianity Continues at Rapid Pace." Oct. 17, 2019. https://www.pewforum.org/2019/10/17/in-u-s-decline-of-christianity-continues-at-rapid-pace/

Pink, Aiden. "Here Are the 17 Members of Congress Who Voted against Condemning BDS." Jul. 24, 2019. https://forward.com/fast-forward/428179/congress-bds-aoc-tlaib-omar/

Rosove, John. "Do You Have to Believe in God to Be a Jew?" Jan. 19, 2018. https://reformjudaism.org/blog/do-you-have-believe-god-be-jew

Scham, Paul and Osama Abu-Irshaid. "Hamas: Ideological Rigidity and Political Flexibility." *United States Institute of Peace*. June 2009. https://www.usip.org/sites/default/files/Special%20Report%20224_Hamas.pdf

Sharp, Jeremy. "US Foreign Aid to Israel." Nov. 16, 2020. https://fas.org/sgp/crs/mideast/RL33222.pdf

Smith, Grant. "Poll: Americans Reject Israeli Annexation." May 18, 2020. https://original.antiwar.com/smith-grant/2020/05/17/poll-americans-reject-israeli-annexation/

Stanley, Brian. "Spreading the Word: The Missionary Expansion of Christianity." Sep. 23, 2019. https://www.bl.uk/sacred-texts/articles/spreading-the-word-the-missionary-expansion-of-christianity#

Telhami, Shibley. "Changing American Public Attitudes on Israel/Palestine: Does It Matter for Politics?" Accessed Oct. 19, 2021. https://pomeps.org/changing-american-public-attitudes-on-israel-palestine-does-it-matter-for-politics

"The Failure of the Oslo Accords." University of California Press. Sept. 27. Accessed Oct. 19, 2021. https://www.ucpress.edu/blog/38369/the-failure-of-the-oslo-accords/

Tourist Israel. "Why Tel Aviv Is the Ultimate LGBTQ Travel Destination." Accessed Oct. 19, 2021. https://www.touristisrael.com/why-tel-aviv-is-the-ultimate-lgbtq-travel-destination/26062/

Washington Report. "US Financial Aid to Israel: Figures, Facts, and Impact." Accessed Oct. 19, 2021. https://www.wrmea.org/congress-u.s.-aid-to-israel/u.s.-financial-aid-to-israel-figures-facts-and-impact.html

Wren, Adam. "Meet the Group Trying to Change Evangelical Minds about Israel." Mar. 10, 2019. https://www.politico.com/magazine/story/2019/03/10/evangelicals-israel-palestinians-telos-225704

Yousef, Ahmed. "Engage with Hamas." *Washington Post.* Jun. 20, 2007. https://www.washingtonpost.com/wp-dyn/content/article/2007/06/19/AR2007061901736.html

CHAPTER 7

Adamson, Peter. "Arabic Translators Did Far More Than Just Preserve Greek Philosophy." Accessed Oct. 19, 2021. https://aeon.co/ideas/arabic-translators-did-far-more-than-just-preserve-greek-philosophy

Baxter, Mary. "Zipporah: The Wife of Moses." Accessed Oct. 19, 2021. https://www.blueletterbible.org/Comm/baxter_mary/WitW/WitW09a_Zipporah.cfm

Bible Reference. "Genesis 17:20 Parallel Verses." Accessed Oct. 19, 2021. https://www.bibleref.com/Genesis/17/Genesis-17-20.html

Elias, Abu. "Hadith on Christ: Muhammad Closer to Jesus Than Anyone Else." Accessed Oct. 19, 2021. https://abuaminaelias.com/dailyhadithonline/2011/05/18/muhammad-closer-to-jesus/

Emir-Stein Center. "Why Evangelicals Hate Muslims: An Evangelical Minister's Perspective | Pastor Bob Roberts Jr." Apr. 29, 2019. https://www.youtube.com/watch?v=opcUsTBkIMA&t=163s

ESL Connexus. "Arabs in the Bible #2: Moses Married an Arab." Apr. 26, 2018. http://www.eslconnexus.com/2018/04/arabs-in-bible-moses-married-arab.html#:~:text=Zipporah%20 is%20thought%20to%20mean,is%20a%20beautiful%20Arabian%20woman.&text=Zipporah%20has%20very%20dark%20skin,marrying%20a%20woman%20of%20color

Grabar, Oleg. "Islamic Jerusalem or Jerusalem under Muslim Rule." *The City in the Islamic World (2 vols.)*. Brill Academic, Jun. 18, 2020. https://brill.com/view/book/edcoll/9789047442653/Bej.9789004162402.i-1500_015.xml

Loeffler, James. "The Problem with the 'Judeo-Christian Tradition.'" Aug. 1, 2020. https://www.theatlantic.com/ideas/archive/2020/08/the-judeo-christian-tradition-is-over/614812/

Lumen Learning. "Pre-Islamic Arabia." Accessed Oct. 19, 2021. https://courses.lumenlearning.com/boundless-worldhistory/chapter/pre-islamic-arabia/#:~:text=One%20of%20the%20major%20cultures,also%20be%20called%20a%20clan

Orthodox Christian Information Center. "St. John of Damascus's Critique of Islam." Accessed Oct. 19, 2021. http://orthodoxinfo.com/general/stjohn_islam.aspx

Seigal, Robert. "Ben Franklin's Famous 'Liberty, Safety' Quote Lost Its Context in 21st Century." Mar. 2, 2015. *All Things Considered*. Podcast. https://www.npr.org/2015/03/02/390245038/ben-franklins-famous-liberty-safety-quote-lost-its-context-in-21st-century#:~:text=Benjamin%20Franklin%20once%20said%3A%20%22Those,and%20concerns%20about%20government%20surveillance

CHAPTER 8

Associated Press in New York. "Lawsuit Brought by Muslims Rounded up after 9/11 Gets Go-Ahead from Court." Jun. 21, 2015. https://www.theguardian.com/us-news/2015/jun/21/lawsuit-muslims-september-11-roundup-abuse

Fisk, Robert. "Sabra and Shatila." Accessed Oct. 19, 2021. https://www.countercurrents.org/pa-fisk180903.htm

Fisk, Robert. "Sabra and Chatila Taught Me All Massacres Become 'Alleged Massacres' If We Don't Pay Attention." Accessed Oct. 19, 2021. https://www.independent.co.uk/voices/robert-fisk-sabra-chatila-genocide-armenia-holocaust-israel-yung-chang-not-movie-a9244401.html

Gerstein, Josh. "Authorities Probe Alleged Abuse of Al-Arian." Apr. 19, 2007. https://www.nysun.com/national/authorities-probe-alleged-abuse-of-al-arian/52836/

Kimball, Jill. "The Cost of the Global War on Terror: $6.4 Trillion and 801,000 Lives." Nov. 13, 2019. https://www.brown.edu/news/2019-11-13/costsofwar

Kutler, Stanley. "Taking on Another President: Judge Damon Keith." Accessed Oct. 19, 2021. http://hnn.us/articles/973.html

Lu, Jackie. "How Terror Changed Justice: A Call to Reform Safeguards That Protect against Prosecutorial Misconduct." Journal of Law and Policy Vol. 14, no. 1 (2005). https://brooklynworks.brooklaw.edu/cgi/viewcontent.cgi?article=1243&context=jlp

Meyer, Josh. "11 Indicated in Suspected Virginia Terrorist Cell." *LA Times*. Jun. 28, 2003. https://www.latimes.com/archives/la-xpm-2003-jun-28-na-indict28-story.html

Ross, Jay. "War Casualties Put at 48,000 in Lebanon." *Washington Post*. Sep. 3, 1982. https://www.washingtonpost.com/archive/politics/1982/09/03/war-casualties-put-at-48000-in-lebanon/cf593941-6067-4239-a453-71bdcaf9eba0/

Royer, Ismail. "Letter of Ismail Royer to Judge Brinkema upon Sentencing." Feb. 2, 2017. https://agoodtree.net/2017/02/02/letter-of-ismail-royer-to-judge-brinkema-upon-sentencing-331/

Shakra, Eyad. "The Sabra and Shatila massacre." Apr. 18, 2020. https://www.arabnews.com/node/1660936

CHAPTER 9

Carroll, Conn. "Colleges Don't Have a Guy Problem. America Has a Marriage Crisis." Sept. 15, 2021. https://www.washingtonexaminer.com/opinion/colleges-dont-have-a-guy-problem-america-has-a-marriage-crisis

Collins, Lois. "What Research Says about Two-Parent Families Keeping Kids Out of Jail and in School." Jun. 17, 2021. https://www.deseret.com/2021/6/17/22538277/what-research-says-about-two-parent-families-keeping-kids-out-of-jail-brookings-aei-family-studies

Gates, Gary. "How Many People Are Lesbian, Gay, Bisexual, and Transgender?" Apr. 2011. https://williamsinstitute.law.ucla.edu/publications/how-many-people-lgbt/

Halpin, Hayley. "'A Gender Equality Paradox': Countries with More Gender Equality Have Fewer Female STEM Grads." Feb 18, 2018. https://www.thejournal.ie/gender-equality-countries-stem-girls-3848156-Feb2018/

Kaufman, Scott. "Taking Sex Differences in Personality Seriously." Dec. 12, 2019. https://blogs.scientificamerican.com/beautiful-minds/taking-sex-differences-in-personality-seriously/

Killian, Anzel. "Top Female CEOs in the UK in 2020." Mar. 18, 2020. https://www.ig.com/uk/news-and-trade-ideas/top-female-ceos-ftse-100#:~:text=In%202020%2C%20only%205%25%20of,which%20means%2095%25%20are%20male

National Center for Education Statistics. "Characteristics of Public School Teachers." May, 2021. https://nces.ed.gov/programs/coe/indicator_clr.asp#:~:text=See%20Digest%20of%20Education%20Statistics,school%20level%20(36%20percent).

Ramble. "Jordan B. Peterson: Why So Many Male Engineers and Female Nurses?" Aug. 27, 2017. Video. https://www.youtube.com/watch?v=d7uZOAzVRgU

Taylor, Dan. "First Muslim Woman Elected to VA School Board Has Big Ideas." Nov. 7, 2019. https://patch.com/virginia/

fairfaxcity/1st-muslim-woman-elected-va-school-board-has-big-ideas

CHAPTER 10

Ahmed, Nilofar. "The Conquest of Makkah." Oct. 28, 2011. https://www.dawn.com/news/669529/the-conquest-of-makkah

Aljazeera. "Former US Soldier Guilty of Rape Found Hanged." Feb. 19, 2014. https://www.aljazeera.com/news/2014/2/19/former-us-soldier-guilty-of-rape-found-hanged

bin Muhammad, Ghazi, Ibrahim Kalin, and Mohammad Hashim Kamali. *War and Peace in Islam: The Uses and Abuses of Jihad*. The Royal Islamic Strategic Studies Centre 2013. https://rissc.jo/books/War-Peace-Islam.pdf

Butt, Ahsan. "Why Did Bush Go to War in Iraq?" Mar. 20, 2019. https://www.aljazeera.com/opinions/2019/3/20/why-did-bush-go-to-war-in-iraq

Cachero, Paulina. "US Taxpayers Have Reportedly Paid an Average of $8,000 Each and over $2 Trillion Total for the Iraq War Alone." Feb. 6, 2020. https://www.businessinsider.com/us-taxpayers-spent-8000-each-2-trillion-iraq-war-study-2020-2

Hamourtziadou, Lily. "Iraq 2020: Legitimacy, Security and War Crime Let-Offs." Dec. 31, 2020. https://www.iraqbodycount.org/analysis/numbers/2020/

History, Art & Archives: United States House of Representatives. "Power to Declare War." Accessed Oct. 28, 2021. https://history.house.gov/Institution/Origins-Development/War-Powers/

Internet Encyclopedia of Philosophy. "Just War Theory." Accessed Oct. 28, 2021. ttps://iep.utm.edu/justwar/#:~:text=The%20principles%20of%20the%20justice,proportional%20to%20the%20means%20used

Karim, Kaleef. "Discover the Truth: Quran 9:5—Sword Verse." Mar. 4, 2014. https://discover-the-truth.com/2014/03/04/quran-95-sword-verse/

Parrott, Justin. "Jihad in Islam: Just-War Theory in the Quran and Sunnah." *Yaqeen Institute of Islamic Research* May 15, 2020. https://archive.nyu.edu/handle/2451/61278

Schorr, Daniel. "War Crimes in Iraq: Haditha and Abu Ghraib." Sep. 2, 2007. Podcast. *Weekend Edition Sunday.* https://www.npr.org/templates/story/story.php?storyId=14124158

Schweitzer, Yoram. "The Rise and Fall of Suicide Bombings in the Second Intifada." *Strategic Assessment* Vol. 13 No. 3, Oct. 2010. https://www.inss.org.il/wp-content/uploads/sites/2/systemfiles/(FILE)1289896644.pdf

Statista. "Number of Documented Civilian Deaths in the Iraq War from 2003 to September 2021." Accessed Oct. 28, 2021. https://www.statista.com/statistics/269729/documented-civilian-deaths-in-iraq-war-since-2003/

Suitt, Thomas. "High Suicide Rates among United States Service Members and Veterans of the Post- 9/11 Wars." Jun. 21, 2021. https://watson.brown.edu/costsofwar/files/cow/imce/papers/2021/Suitt_Suicides_Costs%20of%20War_June%2021%202021.pdf

Wells, Donald. *An Encyclopedia of War and Ethics*. Portsmouth, NH: Greenwood Publishing Group, 1996. http://www2.hawaii.edu/~freeman/courses/phil100/14.%20The%20Ethics%20of%20War%20and%20Peace.pdf

CHAPTER 11

Badary, Osama, Marwa Hamza, and Rajiv Tikamdas. "Thymoquinone: A Promising Natural Compound with Potential Benefits for COVID-19 Prevention and Cure." May 3, 2021. https://www.ncbi.nlm.nih.gov/pmc/articles/PMC8106451/

CDC. "About Chronic Disease." Accessed Oct. 20, 2021. https://www.cdc.gov/chronicdisease/index.htm

Encyclopedia.com. "The Significance of Ibn Sina's Canon of Medicine in the Arab and Western Worlds." Accessed Oct. 20, 2021. https://www.encyclopedia.com/science/encyclopedias-almanacs-transcripts-and-maps/significance-ibn-sinas-canon-medicine-arab-and-western-worlds

Gunnars, Kris. "6 Reasons Why Eggs Are the Healthiest Food on the Planet." April 26, 2018. https://www.healthline.com/nutrition/6-reasons-why-eggs-are-the-healthiest-food-on-the-planet#TOC_TITLE_HDR_3

Kumar, Sampath, Rama Rao, and Ambika Devi. "Comparative Study of Fenugreek Seeds on Glycemic Index in High and Medium Dietary Fiber Containing Diets in NIDDM Patients." January 2011. https://www.researchgate.net/publication/236677852_Comparative_Study_of_Fenugreek_Seeds_on_Glycemic_Index_In_High_And_Medium_Dietary_Fiber_Containing_Diets_In_NIDDM_Patients

May, Ashleigh, David Friedman, Bettylou Sherry, and Heidi M. Blanck. "Morbidity and Mortality Weekly Report (*MMWR*)." CDC. Nov. 22, 2013. https://www.cdc.gov/mmwr/preview/mmwrhtml/su6203a20.htm

CHAPTER 12

Bagby, Ihsan. "The American Mosque 2020: Growing and Evolving Report 1 of the US Mosque Survey 2020: Basic Characteristics of the American Mosque." Jun. 2, 2020. https://www.ispu.org/report-1-mosque-survey-2020/

Chouhoud, Youssef. "To Have and to Hold, Part Two: Interracial Marriage among American Muslims." Jan. 22, 2020. https://www.ispu.org/interracial-marriage-among-american-muslims/

Diamant, Jeff, Besheer Mohamed, and Elizabeth Sciupac. "Muslims More Likely Than Americans Overall to Say Blacks Lack Equal Rights in US" Sept. 18, 2017. https://www.pewresearch.org/fact-tank/2017/09/18/muslims-more-likely-than-americans-overall-to-say-blacks-lack-equal-rights-in-u-s/

Dosomething.org. "11 Facts about Racial Discrimination." Accessed Oct. 24, 2021. https://www.dosomething.org/us/facts/11-facts-about-racial-discrimination

Gal, Shayanne, Andy Kiersz, Michelle Mark, Ruobing Su, and Marguerite Ward. "26 Simple Charts to Show Friends and Family Who Aren't Convinced Racism Is Still a Problem in America." Jul. 8, 2020. https://www.businessinsider.com/us-systemic-racism-in-charts-graphs-data-2020-6#the-unemployment-rate-has-also-spiked-for-all-racial-groups-in-the-us-during-the-coronavirus-pandemic-and-is-especially-high-for-black-americans-2

Gibbons-Neff, Thomas and Eric Schmitt. "Despite Vow to End 'Endless Wars,' Here's Where about 200,000 Troops Remain." Oct. 21, 2017. https://www.nytimes.com/2019/10/21/world/middleeast/us-troops-deployments.html

Kieser, Hans-Lukas. "Minorities (Ottoman Empire/Middle East)." Accessed Oct. 24, 2021. https://encyclopedia.1914-1918-online.net/article/minorities_ottoman_empiremiddle_east#:~:text=The%20Ottoman%20Empire%20was%20the,empire%20in%20Europe%20and%20Asia.&text=The%20CUP%20classified%20the%20Ottoman,nation%20in%20the%20Anatolian%20core

McCarthy, Niall. "US Special Operations Forces Deployed to 70% of the World's Countries in 2016." Feb. 7, 2017. https://www.forbes.com/sites/niallmccarthy/2017/02/07/u-s-special-operations-forces-deployed-to-70-of-the-worlds-countries-in-2016-infographic/?sh=6add8e297343

Oxford Languages. "About Us." Accessed Oct. 24 2021. https://languages.oup.com/google-dictionary-en/

CONCLUSION

Encyclopedia.com. "Origins Of the Industrial Revolution." Accessed on Nov. 14, 2021. https://www.encyclopedia.com/history/encyclopedias-almanacs-transcripts-and-maps/origins-industrial-revolution

Faruqi, Yasmeen. "Contributions of Islamic Scholars to the Scientific Enterprise." *International Education Journal*, 2006, 7(4), 391-399. https://files.eric.ed.gov/fulltext/EJ854295.pdf